Passions and Convictions in Matters Political

Explorations in Moral Psychology

Lior Barshack

University Press of America,® Inc.
Lanham · New York · Oxford

University Press of America,® Inc.
4720 Boston Way
Lanham, Maryland 20706

12 Hid's Copse Rd.
Cumnor Hill, Oxford OX2 9JJ

Printed in the United States of America
British Library Cataloging in Publication Information Available

Library of Congress Cataloging-in-Publication Data

Barshack, Lior.
Passions and convictions in matters political : explorations in moral psychology / Lior Barshack.
p. cm.
Includes bibliographical references and index.
l. Social sciences and psychoanalysis. 2. Political psychology. Title.

BF175.4 S65 B37 2000 320',01'9—dc21 00-061581 CIP

ISBN 0-7618-1825-1 (cloth: alk. ppr.)

™The paper used in this publication meets the minimum requirements of American National Standard for Information Sciences—Permanence of Paper for Printed Library Materials, ANSI Z39.48—1984

Contents

Acknowledgements

Materials for this book were gathered in a number of settings. Some derive from my doctoral thesis, as the form of exposition and argument will often suggest. I am grateful to my teachers at the University of Tel-Aviv for making possible my doctoral research in Oxford. Prof. Chaim Gans, Prof. John Glucker and Prof. Shlomo Shoham have been inspiring and helpful teachers. I would like to express my gratitude to Professor Jim Harris, my supervisor at the University of Oxford, for his trust and helpful comments on my work. I am also grateful to the examiners of my doctoral thesis, Dr. Liz Frazer and Prof. Neil McCormick, for their comments and encouragement. During my stay in Oxford, I had the privilege and pleasure of being a member of Worcester College and enjoying the warm hospitality of its tutors and provost. It is a pleasure to recall in particular the generous assistance and advice of Prof. Francis Reynolds.

I completed the book at the new Interdisciplinary Center, Herzliya, where I teach political and legal philosophy, and at the École-Normale-Supérieure where I spent a few semesters as a post-doctoral research associate. I am grateful to Prof. Uriel Reichman and to Prof. Yoram Shachar for their kind invitation to teach at the Interdisciplinary Center, and to the Center's current dean, Prof. Moshe Bar-Niv, for his continuing support. I am equally grateful to Professor Catherine Colliot-Thélène and other scholars at the École-Normale-Supérieure in Fontenay-aux-Roses, Paris, for their very kind invitation and hospitality. My research could not have been completed, nor began, without the generous support of the Pegasus trust, the Karten trust, Avi foundation, the British government awards program for overseas research students and similar program of the French government. Last but not least, I would like to thank my family and mention the encouragement of my friends and colleagues Mikael Garandeau and Alon Harel.

1. Spheres and Positions in Social Structure: An Introduction

Three positions

What is the difference between left and right? This question often serves as a way of saying there is no difference. Left and right governments in today's West are said to pursue the same policies and to do so for similar reasons. Others dismiss the question on the grounds that there is no single rationale behind the everyday classification of political parties into left and right. The categories of left and right are said to be either vague and open-textured or too complex to be captured in a definition. There are too many political divides to be grouped under a single polarity. The formation of polar political allegiances does not obey a clear principle. However, even if the categories of left and right are, to a certain extent, abstractions, ignoring such a widespread categorization may generate greater abstractions. Political philosophy does not have to formulate a simple dualistic principle, but it must make sense of the left - right opposition which shapes modern identities and sensitivities. It is true that the classification of a political claim as 'left' or 'right' usually relies, to a certain extent, on local, traditional articulations of conflicting social forces. However, this does not exclude the possibility of drawing more general distinctions between left and right according to their characteristic claims, their first principles, or the intersubjective *positions* from which their claims are made.

The following discussion will define and analyze different intersubjective positions to enhance our understanding of left and right political ideals. Three basic socio-political positions will be defined: authoritarianism, reconciliation and alienated liberalism. Each position will be defined as a cluster of recognition-relations between spheres of being and their individual occupants. The following table represents the basic political positions analyzed in this book. In a way, the table could serve as a summary of the book. As always, it is helpful to start with the conclusions.

<table>
<tr><td>Mode of Interaction</td><td>Position</td><td>Recognition in Private Sphere</td><td>Recognition in Civic Sphere</td></tr>
<tr><td>Deviant Communitas</td><td>Authoritarian Personality</td><td colspan="2">-</td></tr>
<tr><td rowspan="2">Social Structure</td><td>Reconciled Political Continuum</td><td>+</td><td>+</td></tr>
<tr><td>Alienated Liberalism</td><td>+</td><td>-</td></tr>
</table>

The table is built around the concepts of position, recognition and spheres of being. Each position is characterized by the recognition its occupants receive or do not receive in the private and civic spheres. It will be argued that the authoritarian position is defined by misrecognition in both private and civic spheres or, more precisely, by a lack of differentiation between the spheres. Misrecognized, barely individuated, the authoritarian personality is banished from both spheres and from social structure, as a whole, seeking structure's permanent destruction ('deviant *communitas*').[1] The authoritarian personality cannot attain the high level of individuation social structure assumes and enjoins.

Occupants of the other two positions are individuated in one or both spheres and inhabit structure safely and comfortably. The reconciled position is characterized by recognition in both spheres. As we proceed further down the table, the differentiation between the two spheres becomes more firmly established. The position of alienated liberalism is characterized by ample recognition in the private sphere alongside

[1] While every social structure institutionalizes 'normative *communitas*', namely, temporary, licensed suspensions of the normative system of identities, such as, rituals and festivals, the authoritarian personality aims to collapse social structure once and for all.

misrecognition in the public civic sphere. While the alienated liberal is not recognized in the civic sphere and does not identify with the hegemonic Father, the reconciled liberal accepts and transmits the authority of the hegemonic patriarchal totem to which he is attached. Political reconciliation and alienation are dictated by one's relationship – either of recognition or of misrecognition – with the patriarchal totem of one's descent group and the latter's position in the constellation of rival domination-seeking totems.

The struggle over political hegemony is a struggle between rival totems within one comprehensive kinship frame, the state. Citizens of a nation-state symbolically make up a kin group within which smaller kin groups and their rival totems (or, sub-totems) are organized.[2] If 'totem' initially referred to the most sacred objects of aboriginal tribes, the totemic function is recognized as much more general.[3] The totem is a name for, and a concrete representation of, the separate identity of the group by which it is revered. The totemic-iconic function can be performed by a sacred object, a symbol, a myth. Totemic authority is conceived as the source of the group's fertility and power. It has to be known as such to all members of the group, accepted by them, and by them alone. Discrete totemic symbols may recur among different groups, but each group has its own family of totemic symbols. The group's totemic system often comprises symbols that originated in its sub-groups, a familiar phenomenon in contemporary multi-cultural societies. This system is dynamic: totems come to the fore and vanish in ways that testify for changes in the group's self-definition *vis-à-vis* other groups and

---

[2] Ample historical evidence suggests that the state originated in the transfer of rights and responsibilities of traditional kin groups to institutions that eventually became state institutions. In classical Athens, for example, only a relative of a victim could prosecute for murder, whereas in modern criminal law, the state is the prosecutor for most offences. Gradually, the state replaced older units of kinship becoming a new, general organization of kinship. The state takes the place of the corporate that framed pre-modern kinship systems. Today, the nation state performs the same functions of traditional kinship units, being, for example, the chief prosecutor, the source of property rights and the most basic and all embracing unit of the kinship system.

[3] The concept of 'totemic function' is Legendre's. It implies a very broad understanding of totemism; there is no longer distinction here between totemism and ancestor worship, for example.

vis-à-vis its own sub-groups.[4] Since the totem represents the group's separateness it is often related to its territory[5] or foundation myths. Freud identified the totem with the primal Father, a fictional common Father that features in the conscious and unconscious mythical heritage of the group. Every member of the group, according to Freud, identifies with the primal Father from the beginning of life.[6] Representations of contemporary civil religions – national flags, celebrations, monuments – can be seen as totemic representations.

The above model classifies personalities from a specific perspective for a specific purpose. It applies only to modern political systems, assumes their structure and welcomes any insight into its multiple and complex historical conditions, such as, the modern state and its public sphere. Despite the fact that the model rests on a distinction between the maternal and paternal spheres, I will not pursue questions of gender theory in the present study, though some of the concepts endorsed bear on such questions. The distinction between the two spheres is, at any rate, not the same as the distinction between femininity and masculinity. The identification of the paternal with the political has to do with the function of the Father as the anchor of separation, whether this function was relegated to the Father by culture or nature. It has been suggested by a variety of authors that separation from the primary bond is secured by the intervention of the Father. According to Lacan, the phallus constitutes and guarantees separation from the mother and between object and sign, that is, representation. The political sphere functions as a (paternal) spectacle of this separation. The paternal aspect of the political is thoroughly theatrical. The power staged in the political spectacle is meant to overcome the powers of the symbiosis. In a series of writings, Clifford Geertz (1980, 1985) described how political authority is fabricated as a sacred, centralized theater of power.[7] The very construction of the political sphere as a transcendent – that is, separate, absent and superior – theatrical stage which "falls from the sky" (Legendre 1997, 91)

---

[4] See Worseley (1955).

[5] "…the various component parts and elements of the social structure – communities, local groups, moieties, sections, and so on down to particular persons – are bound to localities by totemic allegiances, not by economic or political forces." (Fortes 1969, 120)

[6] On mythical identification see Freud (1923a).

[7] *See also* Balandier (1992).

institutionalizes separation. The *separation* of the political from everyday life and from the private sphere constitutes the political stage as well as its principal message.[8]

The concepts that structure the above table may strike readers as faithfully Hegelian. The notions of recognition, reconciliation (*Versöhnung*), spheres of recognition into which human existence is divided, maternal and paternal principles and their correspondence to the private and public spheres, the hinted critique of liberalism as alienated – all have Hegelian origins. While some of these concepts – for example, the concept of recognition – have been crudely extracted from the Hegelian context, some remain perhaps close enough to their Hegelian origin to be deemed interpretations of Hegel. Hegel's acute psychological insights call for synthesis with psychoanalytical concepts. The main theoretical orientation of the following discussion is psychoanalytic. One of the aims of this discussion is to bring together many substantial insights, even at the cost of uprooting them from their original theoretical context. As Erikson said, "a true insight survives its first formulation" (1950, 60). The discussion attempts to make a constructive use of Hegelian and Kleinian ideas within a new model that organizes them. This model evolved out of recognition of the need to supplement the numerous valuable insights contained in the Frankfurt School account of the authoritarian personality by drawing on other intellectual traditions.

According to Adorno, Horkheimer and their co-researchers, the authoritarian personality is formed under the influence of paternal authoritarianism that weakens the ego and produces a stern and exacting super-ego. In the process of constructing the model, an alternative,

---

[8] As a symbol of separation, the father comes to represent individuality and universality, while, according to Hegel, woman stands for particularity, immediacy, concreteness and naturalness: "Thus one sex is mind in its self-diremption into explicit self-subsistence and the knowledge and volition of free universality, i.e., the self-consciousness of conceptual thought and the volition of the objective final end. The other sex is mind maintaining itself in unity as knowledge and volition of the substantive, but knowledge and volition in the form of concrete individuality and feeling.... man has his actual substantive life in the state... Woman, on the other hand, has her substantive destiny in the family, and to be imbued with family piety is her ethical frame of mind." (Hegel 1942, 108) *See also* Hegel (1977c, 446-76). For a feminist discussion and criticism of the distinction between the public and private spheres see Pateman (1987).

Kleinian view of authoritarianism, as a product of maternal misrecognition, was expanded into a threefold, differential definition of political positions through the invocation of Hegel's and Honneth's idea that recognition is established separately in different spheres of interaction. In this way, the three positions were defined as different constellations of recognition and misrecognition in different spheres. This is essentially an interpretive rather than an empirical procedure. The model's claims should be understood as interpretive claims that reflect an attempt to organize in a simple and coherent way existing theories of political psychology and political anthropology, object relations theories and some literary illustrations of the political.

To date, the concept of an individual's social position has been understood in different ways. It can refer to a constellation of power relations, the entirety of one's jurally recognized rights and powers, a location in a "discursive formation" or a place in the network of interrelated social identities (social structure).[9] The present model lays emphasis on the relation between the concept of position and the concept of recognition: position is determined by the constellation of relations of recognition or misrecognition between an individual and different spheres of interaction. Positions crystallize along the process of individuation. According to Mead, roles and identities are formed in an interpersonal process which upholds social structure.

> [T]he process out of which the self arises is a social process which implies interaction of individuals in the group, implies the pre-existence of the group... [T]he self appears in experience essentially as a 'me' with the organization of the community to which it belongs. This organization is, of course, expressed in the particular endowment and particular social situation of the individual. He is a member of the community, but he is a particular part of the community, with a particular heredity and position which distinguishes him from anybody else. He is what he is in so far as he is a member of this community, and the raw materials out of which this particular individual is born would not be a self but for his relationship to others in the community of which he is a part. (Mead 1934, 164, 200) [10]

---

[9] In *The Archaeology of Knowledge* (1976, 52) Foucault speaks of "enunciative positions" that are said to exist prior to the "speaking subject."

[10] It will be assumed that the interpersonal process of the construction of selfhood and social identity Mead describes has psychoanalytical origins and

Honneth has aptly construed the young Hegel's conception of recognition, as manifested in love, solidarity and rights, and adapted this conception to the interests of contemporary social theory. Recognition is a mutual relationship between individuals who respect each other's separateness. The opposition between recognition and misrecognition, definitive of the three positions, distinguishes between relationships that are based on the parties' accomplished separation-individuation and relationships of fusion. Fromm and Klein highlighted the sado-masochistic nature of relations of fusion. As we shall see, social structure is characterized by mutual recognition, and *communitas* – by fusion.

Recognition encourages the establishment of *'secondary' identifications*, that is, identifications that assume and consolidate

---

repercussions. (Mead recognizes the existence of an *I* alongside the *Me*, the communicatively determined identity and position. But this *I* does not constitute and shape the individuals' position as psychoanalytic factors do. It finds expression within a space already defined by the *Me*). Like Mead and Habermas, the present model draws on the concept of recognition but approaches it from a psychoanalytic point of view: relations of recognition or misrecognition with parental figures are seen as shaping one's position and later determining the *selective* course of the communicative formation of identity, which Mead describes. From an intersubjective standpoint – Mead's and Gadamer's, for example – positions would be seen as formed and maintained in interaction: they are defined in relation to each other. Any interaction-context would be seen as an interplay of positions. As one is exposed to and partakes in widening circles of interaction, the interpersonal crystallization of one's position continues. Mead, Gadamer and Habermas describe the ongoing hermeneutic process as an interplay of individual positions and identities, but psychoanalysis may suggest the driving forces and orientations underlying this dialectical interplay of positions. Relations of recognition or misrecognition – initially in relation to one's parents as initial caretakers and representatives of spheres of interaction – result in certain constellations of object-choices and ethical identifications. Such an approach to positions can explain the unity underlying their multiple manifestations: ethical, sexual, political, aesthetic, metaphysical and so on. (This is not an a-historical conception of positions since socio-historical principles both structure early family experiences and determine the further crystallization of a position towards the hegemonic totemic order in the course of social interaction). Later, these early sources of recognition are replaced by ethical communities and institutions to which we are attached, and which lay down conditions of recognition in the form of ideals of the Good. Positive and negative attachments to surrounding ethical traditions that compete for hegemony derive from these early attachments.

separation-individuation.[11] Important identifications that originate in relations of recognition establish, to use Klein's term, a strong good self, which is also Winnicott's "true self" insofar as both are conditioned by positive responsiveness to initiatives. The establishment of a strongly individuated good self, accompanied by the formation of secondary identifications,[12] implies the establishment of differentiation between the private and civic spheres. Maternal recognition establishes, together with strong ego boundaries, two differentiated spheres of existence. Concomitantly, firm recognition-based individuation saves the individual from the authoritarian position. Klein's account of schizoid-paranoid mechanisms – defense mechanisms in the face of maternal misrecognition, such as, split, projection, denial and idealization – will be shown to be essential to our understanding of how authoritarian ego weakness, paranoia and sado-masochism result from maternal misrecognition.

The three positions presented in the diagram are defined as different combinations of relations to the two spheres. Freud and Klein considered differentiated identification with the two parents as a mature identification that resolves the Oedipus complex. With such mature identification the process of individuation and integration reaches a high stage, which facilitates attainment of the reconciled position.

> The broad general outcome of the sexual phase dominated by the Oedipus complex may, therefore, be taken to be the forming of a

---

[11] Fairbairn uses the terms 'primary' and 'secondary identification' in the same way: "I employ the term '*primary identification*' here to signify the cathexis of an object which has not yet been differentiated from the cathecting subject. The unqualified term 'identification' is, of course, sometimes used in this sense; but it is more commonly used to signify the establishment of a relationship based on non-differentiation with an object which has already been differentiated in some measure at least. This latter process represents a revival of the type of relationship involved in primary identification, and should thus, strictly speaking, be described as a '*secondary identification*'. " (1952, 34-35)

[12] Various available sources of recognition might become the object of secondary identification and thus shape the early organization of the object-world, namely, *the constellation of benevolent and malevolent (misrecognizing) objects,* the core of one's position. Klein describes the organization of an integrated object-world as a gradual process involving regressive resorts to schizoid-paranoid mechanisms. Once a stable organization of the object-world is achieved, external objects can support this structure from without.

> precipitate in the ego, consisting of these two identifications in some way united with each other. (Freud 1923a, 34)

According to Klein, a mature object-world should include separate, complete (as opposed to split) and predominantly benevolent representations of the two parents.[13] Such an object-world originates already in the pre-Oedipal stage.

> If the boy can turn some of his love and libidinal desires from his mother's breast towards his father's penis, while retaining the breast as a good object, then his father's penis will figure in his mind as a good and creative organ which will give him libidinal gratification as well as give him children as it does to his mother. (Klein 1945, 411)

Political ideals express value dispositions that are built into various constellations of internal objects. Recognition and misrecognition in the private and civic spheres, that define the three positions, shape fundamental moral attitudes. Mutual recognition in the private sphere translates into the political concern for individual rights and universal welfare. Mueller attributes to Weber the following conception of the "socialist ethos":

> ...as much as capitalism is marked by the market and commodity production for profit, its opposite is marked, not only by monopoly and planning, but also by the household, or *oikos*, as its special 'mode of production'. The latter includes production, not for profit and exchange value but, rather, for the satisfaction of wants (sufficiency) and use value. It is from this goal that both the need for monopoly and planning originates as, up to this date, every family budget demonstrates. We have thus come to the heart of the matter: to conduct a whole economy and society as though they were a single household, with an equal satisfaction of wants for each and for all denotes the 'law of motion' of a socialist society and economy. (Mueller 1982)

From the private sphere comes the liberal-egalitarian conception of the entire society as one household where individual self-assertion, mutual concern and a universal right to welfare coexist. Rawls' theory of justice, insofar as it construes society as a "fair system of cooperation" with "equal concern and respect" for every citizen, constitutes a contemporary formulation of the household ideal. I shall sometimes refer to this conception of society as the household, or *oikos,* paradigm. It

---

[13] As opposed to the archaic combined parental image described in Klein's early work (1950).

considers principles of fairness and restitution as built into the social relation. Fromm, Horkheimer and Winnicott rightly regarded the traditional family structure as an efficient obstacle to authoritarianism because it entrenches a sense of autonomy and sensitivity to welfare.

Let us move from the private to the civic sphere. As an emblem of separation, the Father/father represents the sphere of citizenship and political power. Mature patriarchal identification may develop into an empowering sense of political membership and into identification with leaders that represent normative, totemic authority and identity. Its political expressions may include assertions of the national, of the competitive individual and of traditional models and interdictions.[14] The alienated liberal does not identify with the hegemonic Father, while the reconciled liberal accepts and transmits the authority of the hegemonic patriarchal totem to which he is attached. Identification with the paternal sphere is a seizure of territory, as modest or expansive as it may be, in the social world.[15] In the course of Western history political authority was taken to be derived from paternal authority and revolutionary tendencies were often interpreted as revolts against the Father (Schorske 1973; Schochet 1975; Legendre 1989). For the right, whether or not strictly authoritarian, as well as for the reconciled left, the mythical, totemic lineage – as old as possible – functions as a source of recognition.

Patriarchal recognition conditions identification with the hegemonic totem and reconciled participation in the public sphere.[16] An individual inhabits a sphere of interaction as a separate and integrated person only under conditions of recognition. Without recognition there is regression to schizoid-paranoid defense mechanisms in the misrecognizing sphere of

---

[14] National identity does not indicate identification with the paternal sphere. The nation is often represented by maternal symbols. In a secular and democratic world, the nation remains the only available source of *concrete* identity and *universal* – in a Hegelian sense – participation.

[15] "If one is maintaining his property in the community, it is of primary importance that he is a member of that community, for it is his taking of the attitude of the others that guarantees to him the recognition of his own rights… It gives him his position, gives him the dignity of being a member in the community." (Mead 1934, 199)

[16] Family authority parallels state authority/totem since the symbolic significance of the state is that of an extended descent group. *See* Fortes (1969); Legendre, (1992). The state emerged through the amalgamation of property rights, powers and authorities that were previously vested in clans.

interaction. Freud's and Klein's accounts of paranoia entail that misrecognition – in the authoritarian and alienated positions – produces paranoid political suspiciousness and exaggeration of persecution through projection of one's own aggression. A non-paranoiac relation to a sphere of interaction further implies a good-self propensity to endorse communal values. These attitudes will be illustrated in the analyses of the positions throughout the book.[17]

There is no simple correspondence between the positions defined in the model, political parties and political ideologies. The three positions do not neatly overlap with party lines. The model outlines relations between socio-psychological positions and fairly abstract values and ethical outlooks. Moreover, each position may issue *conflicting* commands of party loyalty to each of its individual occupants, depending on the traditional ideological allegiance of the occupant's social sub-group and on the position of this sub-group in relation to the hegemonic group and to economic power. For example, occupants of the authoritarian and reconciled positions seem to be 'naturally' inclined to reproduce the dominant ideology of their social group regardless of the actual value-system their own personal position entails. In general, children "will be reluctant to break the emotional bond with a parent to whom they are attached, and as a result, they will be willing to adopt the behaviors that fit the parent's values" (Mussen *et al.* 1990, 172). There are reconciled citizens, for example, who may feel very comfortable under a liberal order and have thoroughly liberal intuitions on issues such as sexual morality, abortion and capital punishment, yet would vote for a mildly conservative religious party due to their group identity, or to another deep-seated commitment. The individual is always implicated in a network of conflicting loyalties and commitments. As Lipset wrote,

---

[17] Communal values and values in general cannot simply be seen as components of 'personal identity', as they often are in contemporary moral philosophy, with its rediscovery of identity, the 'self' and community. The question contemporary writers leave unanswered is: *How* different ethical identities – ethical beliefs and value systems – are formed? *Why* certain values appear in certain positions and not in others? The model suggests that position is determined by one's relation (of recognition or misrecognition) to totemic hegemony in one's descent group (broadly conceived), and the latter's position in the constellation of rival domination-seeking groups. One's position *vis-à-vis* totemic hegemony implies either a general attitude of identification with– or distrust of– prevalent communal values.

> In modern society men are subjected to a variety of experiences and pressures which have conflicting political consequences because men have disparate positions in the class structure... Some of their social positions may predispose them to be conservative, while others favor a more leftist political outlook. (Lipset 1960, 240) [18]

In many cases, discrepancies between ideological self-definitions and concrete ethical intuitions do not make life uncomfortable. Stanley Fish makes this point in the course of his ongoing argument for the primacy of practice over theory.[19] Furthermore, what counts as a contradiction from a certain external, abstract and perhaps meta-historical perspective is not necessarily a contradiction from the point of view of the individual's horizon,[20] though some contradictions would certainly be identified as such from the agent's standpoint as well. In some cases, conflicts between an individual's party and group-commitments, interests and ethical intuitions may become acute. The practice of parties to belittle and repress such conflicts and to align all social issues along several fossilized frontiers has provoked one of the major criticisms of democracy's party system.[21]

---

[18] *See also* Nietzsche's *Will to Power* (1968b, 259).

[19] According to Fish (1989, 332-33), "The impulse to reexamine the principles underlying one's practice can be provoked, moreover, by something that is not even within the field of practice: by turning forty, or by a dramatic alteration in one's economic situation, by a marriage or by a divorce. Of course, it can also be provoked by a theory - but not necessarily. That is, you could engage in the exercise of foregrounding your assumptions and even come to see that some of them were incompatible with some piece of your practice and, nevertheless, respond with a shrug and decide to let things be. The man who declares himself committed to the redistribution of authority and the diffusion of power may be an absolute autocrat in the classroom, and when this is pointed out to him or when he points it out to himself, he may mutter something about the limited attention span of today's youth and go on as before. Even when theory (so called) produces self-consciousness, it need not be 'critical'; it need not be the prelude to change."

[20] *See* Winch's (1970) convincing criticism of Evans-Pritchard's characterization of some Zande beliefs as contradictory.

[21] The *locus classicus* on 'stereotyped parties', 'party formalism', 'party regularity' is Ostrogorski (1982, 340ff.).

Recognition, Spheres and Concrete Forms of Life

The private and civic spheres are more than abstract principles of recognition. They designate concrete spaces of being. The self defines itself and expands within these spheres. These spheres extend, demarcate and divide the inter-subjective space Winnicott termed "potential space." Potential spaces open up between a child and its sources of love and recognition, in relation to whom the child's recognized, "true" self separates itself and develops (Winnicott 1960). The potential space is a space of culture and 'creative living', grounded in interpersonal trust (Winnicott 1991).

> Playing implies trust and belongs to the potential space between (what was at first) baby and mother figure, with the baby in a state of near-absolute dependence, and the mother figure's adaptive function taken for granted by the baby (Winnicott 1991, 51).[22]

Private and public spheres of interaction are based on trust, which conditions the possibility of human relations and language.[23] Occupying a sphere implies reconciliation, self-knowledge, freedom and integrity within its confines. The authoritarian personality does not really inhabit

---

[22] The concept of the potential space derives from Winnicott's earlier (1951) concept of transitional phenomena: "The transitional objects and transitional phenomena belong to the realm of illusion which is at the basis of initiation of experience. This early stage in development is made possible by the mother's special capacity for making adaptation to the needs of her infant, thus allowing the infant the illusion that what the infant creates really exists."
The potential space of trust and mutual recognition forms the basis of our perception of the external world. However, I believe that, contrary to Winnicott's suggestion, the potential space is not a space *between* the internal/psychic and external worlds. It is the *life-world*, a lived world out of which the natural and historical worlds emerge as separate totalities. R. Makkreel (1991) describes how the natural world of science and the historical world are articulated out of the "lived world."

[23] Including the language of lies and deception. "Of course, as individuals we can at any time decide to manipulate others, or to act in an openly strategic manner. But in fact not everyone could behave in this way at any time.... Things like the appropriation of tradition or socialization would become impossible." (Habermas 1994, 101) Philosophers of language such as Searle (1969, 57-63) and Davidson (1982, 135, 162) take the requirement of sincerity to be part of the very concept of a speech act.

either of the two spheres. The alienated liberal is at home only in the private sphere, while the reconciled liberal is at home in both.

Hegel believed that an ethical life (*Sittlichkeit*) with mutual-recognition – that is, a potential space – involves immediate and intuitive self-knowledge. Psychoanalysis lends support to the association of firm individuation and recognition with self-knowledge or a moderate use of idealization and repression. According to Hegel, freedom assumes immediate self-knowledge within *ethical life*. As Pinkard summarized Hegel's view of freedom and knowledge within Greek *ethical life*,

> The Greek conception of freedom embodied three items: The individual was free because (1) he knew *what* it was he was doing (his actions were thus immediately intelligible to him), (2) he knew *why* he was doing it (he could cite socially sanctioned reasons for the action), and (3) he *identified* himself with those actions (since he found his self-identity fully constituted by the social roles that he played).... (Pinkard 1994, 188)

In a similar vein, Gadamer considers hermeneutic appeals to tradition and authority to be requisites for self-knowledge and freedom (Gadamer 1975, 248; 1976, 35). Autonomy, if possible, is situated in networks of relationships of recognition and amidst a complex of attachments which underpin selfhood. According to Gadamer, hermeneutic experience in general is essentially *reflexive*: the ongoing reinterpretation and application of tradition – the hermeneutic foundation of all activity – contains a reflexive moment of self-knowledge. One's constantly revised self-knowledge is a reinterpretation of oneself and of one's traditions and spheres of existence. Self-knowledge and knowledge of the other are continuous, as are inner and social alienation.[24] Within its potential space – the spheres within which it is recognized – the self exists *in-itself* and *for-itself*: it knows and confirms itself in its concrete desires and ends. This self-knowledge is the self-certainty Wittgenstein described as "*comfortable* certainty, not the certainty that is still struggling... I would like to regard this certainty, not as something akin to hastiness or superficiality, but as a form of life..." (Wittgenstein 1974, 46).

Since constitutive attachments to spheres of interaction receive expression in the form of ethical ideals, knowledge of oneself as an occupant of such spheres is an ethical self-knowledge, an "action orienting self-understanding" (Habermas 1988, 162), a hermeneutic

---

[24] This Hegelian idea reappears in the early Marx's conception of alienation (Marx 1992, 322-34).

encounter with one's ethical authorities. According to Gadamer's hermeneutics, in the course of our practical engagement with the world, authoritative ethical traditions are constantly interpreted, negotiated and adopted.

Recognition and attachment foster familiarity and harmony with the concrete details of quotidian forms of life. Concrete forms of life are 'zones of familiarity' in the two senses of familiarity: their residents are members of a single extended *family* (a community) and they are thoroughly *acquainted* with the details of their form of everyday life. Zones of familiarity surround their residents with an envelope of unconditional recognition, empathy and integrity. In their concrete forms of life individuals enjoy reconciliation, self-knowledge and aesthetic joy. There, the body is less harshly separated. It is continuous with the space that surrounds it, a narcissistic envelope that operates as a shared maternal body (the Thing). In this light, 'pollution' should be understood as referring to whatever invades the shared communal body.

Concrete forms of life are always traditional. Suffused with ancestral, totemic mythology, they are conceived of as expressions of a continuous tradition. But the religiosity of concrete forms of life differs from the religiosity of the center. Totemic authorities are represented both at the center – in the political spectacle – and in the domestic and peripheral religiosity of concrete forms of life. There, the hegemonic totem is not a welcome guest: concrete forms of life offer other channels for approaching the Thing. Like religious experience, the language and aesthetics of the sphere of familiarity differ from the language and aesthetics of the center. [25]

Deprived of recognition and genuine attachments, the authoritarian personality's attachment to traditional concrete forms of life is contrived. The authoritarian personality fails to turn the surrounding form of life into a source of firm ethical identity and self-knowledge.[26] Reconciled and alienated liberals, by contrast, find self-knowledge, integrity, freedom and familiarity in different social practices.

---

[25] On the aesthetics of zones of familiarity see Bryson (1990).

[26] "...development as increasing concreteness... through the development this concrete becomes explicit to itself and only drives itself outward to this explicitness... only through this movement is the unity truly concrete. This is life as such, whether natural life or the life of the spirit; it is the life of the Idea. The idea is not dead, not an abstract essence." (Hegel 1985, 83)

Structure and *Communitas*

Integrity and familiarity with spheres of interaction and quotidian forms of life are possible only within social structures, as opposed to *communitas*. The distinction between the two orders helps to introduce and clarify various characteristics of the three positions. The deprivations suffered by the authoritarian personality prevent it from rising above a certain minimal threshold, the condition for a secure position within social structure. Various aspects of the authoritarian personality – such as its aversion to the elite and state bureaucracy and the nature of fascist symbolism – are better understood in light of the general nature of 'deviant *communitas*'. I shall sometimes refer to deviant *communitas* as the 'sado-masochistic order', and to social structure as the 'legal-linguistic order'. The authoritarian position constantly aspires to regress to the sado-masochistic order.

Structures are systems of differentiated, mutually defining, concrete normative identities.[27] As Mead writes in a Hegelian vein, " ...there is a social process out of which selves arise and within which further differentiation, further evolution, further organization, take place" (1934, 164). Structural individuation involves the composition of historical and personal narratives of action and responsibility. Through normative narratives – mythical and personal narratives that mirror each other – structure appropriates and disciplines the body. Within structures, concrete normative identities are organized in relation to each other into systems of kinship, divided spheres of life (e.g., family - civil society - state), hierarchical orders and institutionalized rivalries. Social structure, as a whole, is united by a common group identity. Still, structures are articulate, divided. Opposition, struggle over hegemony, oscillation between mutual recognition and self-assertion are inherent to structures. In contrast, the situation of the 'mob' is, according to Mead, a "degradation of social structure" that involves suspension of all social friction and expansion of the self (1934, 213, 218).

Today, the most familiar version of the distinction between structure

[27] Anti normative identities exist in structures, but also they are made possible by the hegemonic normative order.

and *communitas* is the one proposed by Turner (1969).[28] Turner's distinction has had many predecessors, such as the various theories of 'the masses' developed at the turn of the twentieth century to describe crises in structure. The present exposition follows Turner's conceptualizations of structure and *communitas*, albeit with several additions: (a) Structures rest on *mythical foundations*, that is, myths (e.g., foundation myths) that originate in mythical, transitional, structureless periods. With the reemergence of structure, these myths are codified and in their codified form support structure's normative system; (b) Structures give rise to richly concrete traditional forms of everyday life (*zones of familiarity*) and to differentiations between various *spheres of interaction* (e.g., family-market-state), both of which disappear in *communitas*; (c) Structures are further distinguished by a separate, *transcendent* realm of ideals. By contrast, in *communitas*, human existence is *immanent* and complete; there is no *absence*, *desire* or *ideal.*

Turner's distinction needs to be further augmented by a sub-distinction between 'normative' and 'deviant' *communitas*. Every social structure institutionalizes temporary suspensions of the system of normative identities, such as, festivals and rituals. Structure defines spaces and intervals of *communitas* within it by sanctioning certain forms of deviant ritual behavior. Significantly, normative *communitas* remains within the order of structure. While normative *communitas* consists in a licensed and predictable suspension of structure, deviant *communitas* permanently aims at collapsing structure as such rather than merely overthrowing the current hegemonic group, whether temporarily or permanently.

Structural individuation involves alienation. If, for example, urban and market alienation replaced the class alienation of the *Ancien-Régime*, a constant of alienation can be observed. All social structures share this alienation-constant. The high degree of individuation within social structure is anchored in and guaranteed by a legal order of objective categories that command separation and endow the subject with name, gender, rights and duties. Jural categories define the subject by articulating for him spheres of interaction – such as the family – and

---

[28] Hegel's account of *ethical life* (*Sittlichkeit*), while totally disregarded by anthropologists, is probably the most sophisticated theory of structure ever developed.

roles, expectations and obligations within these spheres.[29] Fortes speaks of the 'jural dimension' of kinship classifications, but all identity components have this dimension.[30] Jural categories define the social identity/role of each individual in the name of another legal personality, that of the corporate, the legal personality of the group (kinship group), as a whole. Individual identities within social structure are articulated as organs of social structure.[31] Structural individuation is individuation of organs *vis-à-vis* other organs and *vis-à-vis* the corporate. Only the corporate, as a third agent, anchors the separateness between I and you.

While upholding structure, the law distances itself from spaces of quotidian life within social structure. Firm individuation can be maintained only if, once established by law, it is in certain spheres of life sheltered from direct legal inspection. Within concrete forms of life (zones of familiarity) the imperatives of law and individuation are mitigated to alleviate the burdens of autonomy and responsibility.[32] If individuation involves brutal extraction from the common body and a degree of alienation, in concrete forms of life alienation is mitigated and the individual body is almost fused with the common body. For these reasons, in *communitas* concrete forms of life disappear. In *communitas*, there is no longer need in such compensations that abound in social structures. There, the joys of concrete forms of life seem faint and naive. Zones of familiarity place their residents in the midst of long traditions

---

[29] This can be seen as the jural aspect of the emergence of the subject within the symbolic order.

[30] "The relations of husband and wife, parent and child, sibling and sibling belong not only to the familial domain but also, and at the same time, to the politico-jural domain... If a mother's sister is classified with the mother, this is not because of the adventitious conditioning experience of being partly brought up by her. Nor has it anything to do with the ultimate ends of cultural transmission. It follows from the kind of recognition accorded in the social structure at large to the equivalence that is an inherent property of the sibling relationship." (Fortes 1969, 63, 68)

[31] Every individual can be considered as a 'subsidiary'.

[32] It can be said that the law lays down the basic framework of concrete forms of life and then withdraws. The law intervenes in zones of familiarity only when fundamental, constitutive norms are violated. The law aspires to separate itself from concrete forms of life without ceasing to command individuation-separation within them: legal interventions are required to check the drift towards softening of individual responsibility and towards transgression.

and mobilize daily efforts to the preservation of these traditions. In contrast, *communitas* and its rituals are dissociated from history and daily labor, and infuse participants with self-sufficient, effortless omnipotence.

Concrete forms of life and the hegemonic center are constituted by their distance from each other, a distance that is preserved in stable social structures. A stable social structure is one that tolerates a constant challenging of the norm in the private sphere. Zones of familiarity insist on their distance from the center by allowing mild forms of transgression and unaccountability. The periphery typically insists on being simultaneously part of and separate from the center. Structures place their members within a complex system of similar separations. There are various spheres of interaction *within* structure (family-civil society-state), a clear distinction between structure's inside and outside and a separate politico-religious realm: the political theater of the sovereign collective body. While in structure, as a system of boundaries, the sacred is kept *distant* from the subject, in *communitas* every participant encounters the sacred face to face. The sacred *corporate* personality of social structure is absent.[33] While absence is constitutive of structure, to the result that structure does whatever it can to perpetuate absence, in *communitas* the distance between the immediate and the absent is dissolved. In ceremonies, the direct encounter with the sacred is obedient and reverent as participants temporarily fuse with transcendent authority and mechanically enact its Law without the mediation of their personal, structural identity. In rituals, the encounter is rebellious, the Law is suspended, normative roles and identities – including sexual identity – are reversed (Turner 1969, 95, 102), and aggression is licensed, though usually in mitigated forms, as happens, for example, in football games, festivals, democratic elections and so on.[34]

In *communitas*, the distance between the immediate and the transcendent dissolves. The Sacred is no longer remote. Whereas religion assumes institutionalization (a church), a system of normative social roles and identities, the separation of the individual from the sacred and acceptance of the burdens of normativity, in magic (*communitas*) – in ceremony or in ritual – separation is suspended and replaced by each participant's fusion with sacredness. *To reiterate, in religion the sacred remains transcendent and absent, it is only represented; in magic,*

---

[33] Like the gods, corporate persons are absent and act through representatives.

[34] On the distinction between ritual and ceremony see Turner (1982).

representation is replaced by immediate presence. Religion is an ongoing theater of representation, magic – a fleeting, intense, ecstatic presence of the sacred in ritual or ceremony. It is hardly surprising, then, that magic is usually conceived as anti-normative and arouses religion's suspicion. Religion exists in the routine of social structure, a routine in which a distance is maintained between everyday life and a well-delimited sphere of the sacred. This distance disappears in ceremonies and rituals. Durkheim and Mauss distinguished magic from religion as being non-institutionalized, private and anti-normative. While magic is indeed anti-normative and non-institutionalized, it may sometimes be endorsed by the community as a whole during ecstatic, collective suspensions of normativity.

The order of normative boundaries and spheres is usually understood to be at war with desire. This assumption, which seemed central to thinkers such as Deleuze and Foucault, may on a certain level be valid. However, the normative order appears to be built into desire and not only opposed to it. Desire emerges in individuals confined to the boundaries of the normative system of structure. This is a point that Lacan emphasized and which should be integrated into the theory of structure: structures contain law – a normative system – and desires and ideals which are inseparable from this normative system. According to Lacan,

> The dialectical relationship between desire and the law causes our desire to flare up only in relation to the Law, through which it becomes the desire for death. It is only because of the law that sin – which in Greek means lack and non participation in the Thing – takes on an excessive, hyperbolic character. (1992, 84)[35]

Structures are further characterized by a social organization of labor – something impossible in *communitas* – and by rational and traditional, as opposed to charismatic, leadership. In the romantic thinking on *Bildung*, labor was taken to be the driving force of individual development and emancipation. Individuation and self-consciousness emerge through labor

[35] While needs, according to Lacan, can be fulfilled, desire is never exhausted and constitutes the subject in constant dependence and suspense. Desires represent an eternal quest that is built into the dynamic constitution of the subject in structure, existing outside himself. For another approach see Deleuze and Parnet (1977,125): "Les trois contresens sur le désir sont: le mettre en rapport avec le manque ou la loi; avec une réalité naturelle ou spontanée; avec le plaisir ou, même et surtout, la fête." *See also* Deleuze (1991).

and depend on it for their maintenance. The individual process of individuation-through-labor is only possible as part of a general, social cycle of labor. As Adorno and Horkheimer argued in *The Dialectics of Enlightenment*, labor dictates the organization of public life and sustains social reason, cooperation and the development of culture.

As opposed to structure, *communitas* involves a suspension of individuality and concrete identity. Consequently, social tensions between persons of different or similar status disappear, since status as such vanishes, causing an expansion of the self. The alienation-constant that in structure separates man from his own and other selves is replaced by fusion.

> Essentially, *communitas* is a relationship between concrete, historical, idiosyncratic individuals. These individuals are not segmentalized into roles and statuses but confront one another rather in a manner of Martin Buber's 'I and Thou'. Along with this direct, immediate, and total confrontation of human identities, there tends to go a model of society as a homogenous, unstructured *communitas*, whose boundaries are ideally coterminous with those of the human species. (Turner 1969, 131-132)

As *communitas* precipitates the breakdown of ego boundaries and individuality, individuals are absorbed into the collective self. As a result of the suspension of identities, *communitas* "involves the whole man in his relation to other whole men.... Relations between total beings are generative of symbols and metaphors and comparisons; art and literature are their products rather than legal and political structures" (Turner 1969, 27). Accordingly, populist movements aimed to annihilate structure and establish communication between total, unspecialized human beings.[36] The decline of the cognitive functions of language and the profusion of symbols derive from the suspension of boundaries: "The symbol ends by being confused with the thing it represents..." (Silone 1964, 28, 113). This is Hanna Segal's concept of "symbolic equation" (of object and sign). The maternal recognition that establishes individuation-separation is the foundation of language[37] and of the concomitant system of rights and obligations – since recognition implies rights – which define structure.

---

[36] "Individuals in [simple] societies are competent to fill many roles: they are 'many-faceted', and therefore various, realized and integral personalities." (MacRae 1969, 159)

[37] This is the view of Bion, Segal and Winnicott.

Authoritarian aspirations to evade the burdens and responsibilities of structure and individuality are realized in *communitas*. The authoritarian personality aims towards the collapse of structure as it is dominated by misrecognizing, persecutory objects that hamper its individuation-separation. Several writers on authoritarianism – notably Fromm – identified its sado-masochistic nature. Fromm and Klein identified the sado-masochistic nature of primary relations of fusion, as opposed to relations between mutually recognizing separate individuals. In *communitas*, primary sado-masochistic fusion replaces individuation as the persecutory – rather than benevolent – aspect of the maternal imago is enacted.[38] In contrast to the paranoid-schizoid and sado-masochistic order of ritual, established by the ascent of the persecutory maternal imago, the legal-linguistic order of structure rests on maternal recognition that secures individuation and firm ego boundaries. While social structure extracts the individual body from the collective body and projects this sacred collective body onto a transcendent, distant, separate sphere, in the authoritarian ritual all participants dissolve into a single (maternal) body.

Social structure is a collective achievement in which strongly individuated persons mutually recognize each other's differentiated identity. Structure seduces them to resist certain forms of violence and fusion. Maternal recognition, which conditions separation-individuation and the possibility of mature identifications, is also a condition for mutual recognition between mature persons within social structure. This claim reiterates Hegel's indication that mutual recognition involves the emergence of a collective, Third point of view: the viewpoint of Spirit and of the state as the epitome of Spirit. According to Hegel and Mead, individuals mutually recognize each other through their objective roles in social structure. Structure replaces the primary symbiotic bond, being another benevolent Absolute Other within which the individual self is absorbed. The identification of the imago underlying the group as maternal rather than paternal has been suggested by Bion. "My impression is that the group approximates too closely, in the minds of the individuals composing it, to very primitive fantasies about the contents of

---

[38] Sado-masochistic elements are prominent in body art and performance art, which are forms of anti-hegemonic ritual in contrast to both bourgeois theater and the *established* avant-garde, which remain within the hegemonic order. See, for example, the masochistic elements in performances of Chris Burden, Stellarc and Marina Abramovitch (Schimmel 1998).

the mother's body."[39] The maternal imago underlying firm structure is predominantly benevolent while the one underlying *communitas* – predominantly malevolent. Culture, forms of everyday life, zones of familiarity can be said to be *selfobjects* replacing primary symbiotic attachment while, at the same time, sustaining the process of individuation and self-discovery by absorbing related anxieties and providing consolations for lost symbiosis. For well-individuated, non-authoritarian, personalities, social structure and its zones of familiarity form, to use Bion's term, a maternal "container."[40]

While "...social structure is intimately connected with history" (Turner 1969, 153), the time of *communitas* and ritual is 'mythical time', a time outside ordinary historical chronology or the chronology of deliberation and action (Eliade 1954; Turner 1985; Falassi 1987). In other words, mythical time is pre-historical in that society relapses during *communitas* to its mythical, founding period, before its normative framework was laid down. In the end, mythical time gradually transforms into history, which starts afresh by relegating the sacred events and figures of mythical time to a separate (transcendent) realm, in the form of timeless, mythical, two-dimensional figures and narratives. Since both 'rational' and 'traditional' authorities assume historical consciousness, leadership in *communitas* is charismatic. Such leadership is anti-hegemonic, replacing the structural leadership modeled on authority-

---

[39] According to Bion (1961, 162), the "basic assumptions" of groups correspond to modes of relation to the mother. He writes: "It will be seen from this description that the basic assumptions now emerge as formations secondary to an extremely early primal scene worked out on a level of part objects, and associated with psychotic anxiety and mechanisms of splitting and projective identification such as Melanie Klein has described as characteristic of the schizoid-paranoid and depressive positions" (1961,164).

[40] Fortes suggests in *Kinship and The Social Order* (1969, 172) an aspect of social structure – the corporate – which supports its identification as a maternal container. "Thus when the Ashanti define the lineage as being 'one person' they are thinking of it as if the founding ancestress were eternally present in her descendants, multiplied and replicated but still one and the same, much as a tree (to which a lineage is often compared) is the same tree however many branches it proliferates." Fortes continues: "Full matrisiblings are 'one person', 'of one womb', a corporate unit in the narrowest sense, and sibling succession expresses the recognition of this indivisible corporate identity of the sibling group in opposition to the total lineage." (1969, 175)

and recognition-relations within the traditional family. Luc de Heusch (1987) distinguished between two paradigms of leadership: magical leadership, where authority depends on heroic exploit – such as slaughter of the predecessor – and leadership that derives its authority from succession. The former corresponds to *communitas*, the latter to structure. Under magical leadership, for example, in a fascist régime, the relationship between leader and group is modeled on sado-masochistic symbiosis. According to Anzieu (1984), the charismatic leader in such groups is identified on the fantasy level with the persecuting maternal imago. Where authority rests on succession, the leader – *the political theater* – guarantees normative separation and transcendence of the Thing. His authority – unlike that of the divine king – derives from the law and is bound by the law. The relations between rational authority and its subjects and between every two subjects under rational authority are based on firm separation-individuation.

Already on the descriptive, phenomenological level it can be observed that, in both structure and *communitas*, horizontal relations between individuals reproduce the relation between the group and its leader. The horizontal and the vertical axes mirror each other. In structure, there is firm separation between individuals as well as between the group and its leader. In *communitas*, non-separation between the group, as a whole, and its populist-charismatic leader infects all interpersonal relations.

Structure	***Communitas***
Rational –Traditional	Chrismatic – Populist
Authority	Authority
↑	↓
Individual A ←→Individual B	Individual A →← Individual B
(relations of separation/transcendence)	(relations of fusion)

The mythical time of *communitas* is timelessness, permanent immediacy, a total time like the total beings that inhabit *communitas*. Mythical time is self-sufficient, careless and ignorant of past and future. It is a time of total actualization and non-separation (Thingness), of *jouissance*, of transcendence brought down to earth. In this sense, *communitas* lacks a transcendent mythical foundation – a transcendent narrative – of the kind that serves in structure as a constitutive frame for historical consciousness and for the normative system. Instead of resting on extant codified mythology, *communitas* manufactures new mythologies. As time vanishes, salvation and revelation are immediate, not distant promises. *Communitas* tolerates no lack, limit, or clothing, and therefore no desire or ideal. Consequently, in *communitas*, there is no longer a need for the type of surrogate satisfactions, consolations and compensations that abound in structure. Here, the joys of concrete zones of familiarity seem faint and naive. The transcendent – death – is brought closer and made immediately present. If *communitas* longs for the end of desire, for the withdrawal of libido, it must long for death and self-destruction, too. To use Lacan's distinction, *communitas* is not a time of pleasure but of *jouissance*, associated by Lacan with death and with a realm beyond desire.

The following three chapters share a similar structure. Each begins with an introductory description of the position to which it is devoted, followed by an exposition of the psychoanalytic or Hegelian concepts that inspired the opening description. These expositions are condensed, selective and controversial. They are not meant to provide systematic historical surveys but to enrich the general model by exploring its theoretical sources and selectively incorporating various insights. The book proceeds in a kind of double movement, alternating between more or less organized presentations of the positions and excursions to the theories which inspired their definitions.

2. The Position of the Authoritarian Personality

Many things will have to be destroyed in order to construct the New Order; now we know that Germany also was one of those things. We have given more than our lives, we have sacrified the destiny of our beloved Fatherland. Let others curse and weep; I rejoice in the fact that our destiny completes its circle and is perfect. An inexorable epoch is spreading over the world. We forged it, we who are already its victims. What matters if England is the hammer and we the anvil, so long as violence reigns and not servile Christian timidity? If victory and injustice and happiness are not for Germany, let them be for other nations. Let heaven exist, even though our dwelling place is hell. I look at myself in the mirror to discover who I am, to discern how I will act in a few hours, when I am face to face with death. My flesh may be afraid; I am not. ***Borges, Deutsches Requiem***

The Position of the Authoritarian Personality

The authoritarian position is distinguished from the other two positions by failure of maternal recognition. According to Klein, maternal recognition enables the infant to grow out of primary fusion (the schizoid-paranoid position) and then identify with its mother as a separate individual and prepare itself for a parallel process in relation to the paternal sphere. Maternal recognition involves love, responsiveness, respect and admission of incompleteness on the part of the mother. The recognizing mother allows enough space to be claimed and occupied by the infant and by other spheres.[1]

In the absence of maternal recognition, the authoritarian personality is unable to establish a true differentiation between the two spheres. The authoritarian personality does not lead a divided existence, as if it were constantly in a state of *communitas*. Since the two spheres exist only in their differentiation and polarity, the authoritarian personality knows none of them, neither intimacy nor universality. Authoritarian régimes, such as Nazi Germany, demonstrate how boundaries between the two spheres fade away. Nazi politics invades the family, subjugates it and takes over its functions. The *führer* claims not only the role of The Father, but replaces concrete fathers. The family is no longer autonomous and unaccountable, but is thoroughly transparent and disciplined. The collapse of boundaries between the spheres implies the disintegration of individuation and transcendence,[2] all resulting from maternal misrecognition.

Today, an elimination of boundaries between public and private is advocated by communitarianism. Communitarians do not conceive of the state as a sphere where individuals interact as 'abstract' citizens, that is, with disregard to their concrete communal identities. Communitarians believe that the state is merely an extension and an instrument of the

---

[1] Chasseguet-Smirgel analyzes the infant's turn towards the paternal sphere as a means for liberation from the early exclusive rule of the omnipotent mother. "Thus, women as well as men constantly fear castration: even if they already have lost the *penis*, there are still many other things with a phallic meaning which one might lose. And men as well as women experience penis envy because each attempt to compensate a deficiency implies a phallic acquisition. The fear of loss or of castration centers in the mother as it is from her the daughter wishes to escape, *at the same time that she gives herself a penis and turns to the father*." (1981, 116-17)

[2] On totalitarianism as the collapse of transcendence see Lefort (1986). As the diagram contrasting charismatic and rational authority suggests, the ego boundaries that constitute firm individuation in social structure are the same boundaries that separate the transcendent from the earthly sphere. As Freud implies in *Moses and Monotheism*, in Judaism (and, it can be added, Protestant Christianity) this correspondence between firm transcendence and firm individuation in visible. The boundary that is laid between the ego and the symbiotic bond makes the symbiotic bond transcendent. The origin of individual separation as well as the big Other's transcendence is the primary bond as a whole - a predominantly loving one - rather than the separateness and Otherness of the Father, of death, of the castrated/deprived phallus, or of the signifier.

community and that any attempt to bracket communal identities in the public sphere is both futile and wrong. The communitarian interpretation of democracy is a dangerous, anti-legal interpretation, which presents democracy as an immanent totality devoid of a separation between state and community. Communitarian ideals express the longing for suspension of social structure in the form of *communitas*. By contrast, the republican and liberal interpretations of democracy emphasize the separateness of public and private. Structural individuation is conditioned by the separation between public and private. It is the public, as a separate realm, which extracts the individual from the symbiotic embrace of the familiarity zone, where all participants are extensions of a single (maternal) body (the Thing). While the liberal state constitutes and guarantees individuation by instituting universal principles that disregard the communal affiliation of their subjects, communitarianism threatens individuation by expanding the sphere of community and absorbing the state in the community.[3] The liberal state endows the individual with rights and duties irrespectively of his communal affiliation, thus, securing his position *vis-à-vis* the community. Furthermore, in the liberal public sphere, it is the abstract individual citizen that is institutionalized and recognized as the reflexive and autonomous addressee of open public discourse. Finally, it is the civic sphere as a *mise-en-scène* of *patriarchal* law and power that checks the drift towards communal suspension of norms and boundaries, functioning as an emblem and anchor of individuation-separation.

According to Klein, maternal misrecognition consolidates strong inner persecutory objects, causing a weakening and isolation of the good self and a general failure of individuation. The authoritarian personality is characterized by submission to dominant bad objects, too big, too strong and sometimes too seductive to be disarmed. The authoritarian object-world is dominated by persecutory objects which do not allow development out of primary fusion towards individuation and mature

---

[3] As Legendre writes, "[i]f one reflects upon totalitarian techniques, one discovers that they all monotonously depend upon the elimination of what, in European history, constitutes the *staging of the limit* for the purposes of Reference itself: the distinction between what is public and what is private, the central notions of the theory of jurisdiction around which the genealogical power of the State was formed, *are the guarantee of the reproduction of the subject.* The bond of speech in our culture is lodged on the rock of the division between public and private..." (Legendre 1997, 178)

identification. Chasseguet-Smirgel described authoritarian failures of mature identification and their political consequences:

> Models, in so far as there are any, would be distant and abstract. When they are personified it would not be in someone representing an idealized father substitute but in someone, precisely, who had himself succeeded in avoiding introjective conflicts and in conferring upon himself a magic, autonomous phallus or someone who promises this to his followers whilst sparing them the painful process of development. We have already met such a figure: the 'ideological' leader such as I have attempted to describe in relation to the group… the 'ideological' leader is someone who can make the illusion – the promise of a coming together of ego and ideal – sparkle. (1985, 114)

Maternal persecution and the resulting fear and hatred of the mother are amply represented in authoritarian symbolism. Marinetti's first *Futurist Manifesto* of 1909 makes the following declarations:

> 9. We will glorify war – the world's only hygiene – militarism, patriotism, the destructive gesture of freedom-bringers, beautiful ideas worth dying for, and scorn for woman.
>
> 10. We will destroy the museums, libraries, academies of every kind, will fight moralism, feminism, every opportunistic or utilitarian cowardice. (1971, 42)

Klaus Theweleit's *Male Fantasies* thoroughly documents authoritarian hatred and fear of women. Referring to a large number of Nazi novels, Theweleit answers the following question in the affirmative: "In all these texts, could it be that the fear of dissolution through union with a woman actually causes desire to flee from its object, then transform itself into a representation of violence?" (1987, 45) Authoritarian men feel threatened by the presence of women: "As the woman fades out of sight, the contours of the male sharpen...." (1987, 35) Theweleit seems right to insist that "...even apparently harmless manifestations of the mother-son relationship, like that between the white nurse and wounded soldier, might also be screens for latent aggression toward the mother" (1987, 100).[4]

The persistence of primary fusion (schizoid-paranoid position) in the authoritarian personality as a result of maternal misrecognition accounts

---

[4] Authoritarian resentment of the mother may also underlie, in some cases, objection to abortions, an ethical issue where relations to the private sphere are transparently reflected.

for authoritarian sado-masochism. Like the alienated liberal, whose dependence upon schizoid-paranoid projective mechanisms is nonetheless more moderate, the authoritarian personality *defines* itself by its opposition and disapproval of certain groups. Authoritarian masochism manifests itself in admiration of the strong, self-hate and self-destruction. The authoritarian personality interprets human relationships in terms of domination and submission and places itself in one of these poles.[5] "Just as his 'love' is automatically aroused by power, so powerless people or institutions automatically arouse his contempt." (Fromm 1941, 168)[6]

Masochism has been interpreted both as a form of control of the misrecognizing persecutor and as communicating seduction, appeasement and appeal for mercy (Freud 1919; Bak 1946; Berliner 1958). Masochistic identification with the persecutor internalizes misrecognition and (self) hate. "[A] sense of guilt is invariably the factor that transforms sadism into masochism." (Freud 1919, 189)[7] At the same time, individuality, however servile, is fought for and achieved through compliance. The libidinization of violence perpetuates both submission and survival.[8] Freud further suggests that masochism is a way of coping with anxiety over an anticipated punishment by inflicting the punishment on oneself in advance. In addition, sado-masochism may be a form of control over one's own provoked and unmitigated aggression in that one identifies with it and thereby ostensibly integrates it.

The authoritarian personality can be seen as constantly striving to regress to the sado-masochistic order of *communitas* by collapsing structure. In contrast, firmly individuated personalities need social structure, as a network of mutually defining and mutually recognizing concrete identities, to preserve their individuation (as much as social structure depends on the availability of a sufficient quantity of

[5] On authoritarianism as preoccupation with domination see Fromm (1984, 209-210), *The Authoritarian Personality* (Adorno *et al.* 1950), and Frenkel-Brunswick and Sanford (1946, 114).

[6] "For the sadistic character there is only one admirable quality, and that is power." (Fromm 1975, 325)

[7] Later (1920), Freud believed that masochism can be primary.

[8] "This being beaten is now a convergence of the sense of guilt and sexual love. *It is not only the punishment for the forbidden genital relation, but also the regressive substitute for that relation...*" (Freud 1919, 189)

individuated personalities with determinate differentiated normative identities and roles). While for the non-authoritarian personality social structure functions as a source of maternal recognition that sustains its individuation – namely, as a good maternal "container" – the authoritarian personality identifies structure with the misrecognizing, ferocious maternal imago.

The authoritarian personality resents traditional institutions, elite and elite culture as manifestations of stable structure.[9] In its attacks on elite capital and bureaucracy, authoritarian populism often feigns to be socialist but loses none of its destructiveness.[10] In Israel, Begin's career rested on incessant defamation of the establishment. When Le-Pen's racism in France proved to repel many potential voters, Le-Pen turned to mock the bureaucracy. An enlightened state bureaucracy – Hegel's universal, executive class – epitomizes structure. It is a source of concrete, differentiated identities and the embodiment of humanist traditions. It has to be distinguished from authoritarian hierarchy where participants melt into roles that allow them to act out sadistic fantasies. The hierarchic rigidity of authoritarian bureaucracy only testifies for its inherent weakness, for its being ritual rather than structure. In authoritarian bureaucracy there is no role-distance – no distance between a public and a private body – due to the absence of a private sphere and firm individuation in general. Under fascism, private bodies are thoroughly fused with the collective body. Formal uniform and nakedness are predominant and interchangeable elements in sado-masochistic fantasy in the absence of a relaxed and secure sense of structural identity. Authoritarian bureaucracy is possible only as war. War, a third social modality combining structure and *communitas*, enables the authoritarian personality to realize sado-masochistic fantasies while ostensibly

---

[9] On populist resentment of the elite and state bureaucracy see MacRae (1969, 162). Fromm (1984, 43) identifies a category of authoritarian voters who vote left because of their hatred of elite. Populism fails to give itself a structure. "Populism is in each case loosely organized and ill-disciplined: a movement rather than a party." (Wiles 1969, 167)

[10] The *mouvement de citoyens* in France constitutes a contemporary example. Wiles (1969, 178) is right to claim that populism is closer to fascism than to socialism. It was a pseudo-socialist vengeful crowd that made Nietzsche and Freud anxious about socialism in general, and worried staunch socialists like Fromm, as well.

maintaining order and fighting in the name of traditional values.[11]

Like institutionalization, labor and production assume structural individuation. Accordingly, fascism has been described as anti-production, production of death and misrecognition (Theweleit 1987, 221ff.). The holocaust as a mass-industry of death is the ultimate authoritarian ritual, where totemic-patriarchal laws of morality and representation – embodied by the Jews – were the real objects of annihilation. The nature of *symbolization* also changes under fascist *communitas*. The eruption of symbolism under fascism is often seen as a result of the striving to return to primary fusion, suspend ego-boundaries and reality testing and immerse oneself in the symbol. Hanna Segal has termed such reified symbols "symbolic equations." Segal, Bion and Winnicott have described, in different ways, the dependence of proper symbolization on secure maternal attachment, a bond of which the authoritarian personality is deprived. According to Winnicott (1951; 1960, 146), the mother, functioning as a transitional object, prepares the infant to the acceptance of reality and to the concomitant capacity for symbol formation. According to Bion (1967), a good maternal figure functions as a good "container" and enables the infant to survive bad experiences, represent them and accept reality. Symbolization assumes separation from the symbolized object and separation assumes in turn maternal recognition.

In her early paper, "Notes on Symbol Formation," Segal traced symbol formation to the acceptance of separation and reality during the development out of primary fusion (the passage to the "depressive position"):

> The symbol proper... is felt to *represent* the object; its own characteristics are recognized, respected, and used. It arises when depressive feelings predominate over the paranoid-schizoid ones, when separation from the object, ambivalence, guilt, and loss can be experienced and tolerated. The symbol is used not to deny but to overcome loss. When the mechanism of projective identification is used as a defense against depressive anxieties, symbols already formed and functioning as symbols may revert to symbolic equations. (Segal 1986, 57)

Later, Segal adjusted her views to Bion's findings. Her conclusions capture the origins of fascist symbolism:

---

[11] The alienated liberal's anti hegemonic tendencies are opposite: he often criticizes bourgeois values overtly while remaining committed to social structure.

> Symbolism originates in projective identification, first of all in the relationship to the breast then to the mother's whole body. When this projection results in mutual damage or an excessively omnipotent identification of a 'sticky' kind, symbols formed are excessively concrete, empty of meaning or bizarre. (Segal 1997, 47)

Whereas concrete normative identities are established and arranged within structure, the authoritarian personality does not have an easy sense of identity.[12] The authoritarian personality fails to create a "potential space" and to develop it into a cultural space of integrity and familiarity, of self-knowledge and being-at-home. Such spaces, which rest upon maternal recognition, flourish within firm social structures.[13] Authoritarianism envies structure and seeks its destruction. Authoritarian politics is sado-masochistic and preoccupied with bare power. It is a politics of revenge of real and imagined misrecognition. It reproduces misrecognition in a perpetual and vicious circle. Aggressive foreign policy, punitive inclinations and the formal rationality of economic libertarianism express authoritarian vengefulness. On the other hand, authoritarianism cannot renounce the hope of truly becoming a part of social structure and its hegemonic traditions. It often constructs alternative, fragile structures and claims them to be the true descendants of society's authentic way of life. This is the authoritarian *pseudoconservatism* described by Adorno.

The maternal attitude responsible for the continuing domination of the bad object has been described in a variety of ways. The description of the authoritarian personality so far relied extensively on Kleinian concepts. According to Klein, persecutory objects exist from the start of life and reify destructive drives and one's experiences of frustration. In authoritarianism, an infrastructure of rudimentary object relations

---

[12] The respective roles of social models and of the ethical structure of the object-world in the formation of ethical identity are not frequently addressed. Benjamin (1977a) argues that ethical identity evolves without "internalization." Benjamin's position seems to me to assume an overstated dichotomy between the inner and the outer. The internal object-world crystallizes in relation to external objects which shape and sustain it. The authoritarian personality's object-world perpetuates a failure to internalize recognition-providing value systems.

[13] Spaces of familiarity and integrity cannot be maintained under certain authorities (Fromm 1941, 237-38). The entire mode of being has to change when the nature of authority changes so radically.

continues to dominate the object-world. By contrast, maternal love and responsiveness strengthen the good objects and the ego, thereby creating an object-world that is predominantly benevolent. Maternal recognition prevents the formation of a tyrannical object-world by fostering a deployment of the instincts that is conducive to individuation and integration.

> If the good object is deeply rooted, the split is fundamentally of a different nature and allows the all-important process of ego integration and object synthesis to operate. Thus a mitigation of hatred by love can come about in some measure and the depressive position can be worked through. As a result, the identification with a good and whole object is the more securely established; and this also lends strength to the ego and enables it to preserve its identity as well as a feeling of possessing goodness of its own. (Klein 1957, 192)

According to Bion, the good breast of the recognizing mother accepts the infant's projected bad parts and turns them into good, loving parts that can be then reintrojected. The introjected good parts allow the infant to cope with its aggression more independently.

Klein's approach is usually contrasted with Freud's drive theory, on the one hand, and with other theories of object relations that trace bad objects and aggression exclusively to misrecognition, as opposed to destructive drives,[14] on the other. Freud and Klein agree that some destructiveness is natural. Destructiveness can be provoked and fuelled but it does not have to be imported from without. According to Freud, and contrary perhaps to the Frankfurt School model of paternal authoritarianism, even the level of severity of the super-ego does not directly reflect the severity of the external object.[15]

As opposed to Freud and Klein, Fairbairn traces internal bad objects solely to parental misrecognition. He posits that the internal bad object is formed by an introjection, on the infant's part, of parental aggression. The infant introjects this aggression to exonerate the parent. The bad object originates in the infant's need to protect the goodness of his parents. Fairbairn succeeds in explaining self-destructiveness without assuming

---

[14] *See* Benjamin (1977a).

[15] "...the original severity of the super-ego does not – or does not so much – represent the severity which one has experienced from it [the object], or which one attributes to it; it represents rather one's own aggressiveness towards it." (Freud 1930, 129-30)

Freud's and Klein's hypothesis of the death instinct. While Klein was acutely aware of the threats of annihilation experienced by infants, she did not hold the view that such unmitigated threats can be internalized and entrench mortal self-destructiveness without the assistance of the death instinct.

According to Winnicott – who discussed other aspects of maternal deficiency, as well – maternal misrecognition consists mainly in unresponsiveness to the infant's "spontaneous gestures." From the very beginning, the infant is forced to conform to expectations at the expense of developing a "true," inner self. The outer "false" self is a defensive construction aimed at shielding the weak true self. By contrast, maternal recognition involves willingness to confirm the infant's illusion of omnipotence.

> ...the gesture indicates the existence of a potential True Self.... The mother who is not good enough is not able to implement the infant's omnipotence, and so she repeatedly fails to meet the infant's gesture; instead she substitutes her own gesture which is to be given sense by the compliance of the infant. This compliance on the part of the infant is the earliest stage of the False Self, and belongs to the mother's inability to sense her infant's needs... In the first case the mother's adaptation is good enough and in consequence the infant begins to believe in external reality which appears and behaves as by magic (because of the mother's relatively successful adaptation to the infant's gestures and needs), and which acts in a way that does not clash with the infant's omnipotence. (Winnicott 1960, 145-146)

Horkheimer and the authors of *The Authoritarian Personality* traced authoritarianism to lack of warmth and rationality. As Frenkel-Brunswick (1954, 236) writes on the provision of care, "...warmer, closer and more affectionate interpersonal relationships prevail in the homes of the unprejudiced children...". Lack of rationality usually assumes the form of strict enforcement of an arbitrary or hypocritical system of rules and rewards (Adorno *et al.* 1950, 371). "What seems to count most is the establishment of an intelligible, non-ego-destructive type of discipline..." as opposed to "the expectation of a quick learning of external rigid and superficial rules..."

> The lack of an internalized and individualized approach to the child on the part of the parents and the tendency to transmit mainly a set of fixed rules and customs may be considered as interfering with the development of a clear-cut personal identity and integration in the growing child. (Frenkel-Brunswick 1954, 236,239)

Kafka's famous letter to his father illustrates clearly the effects of parental arbitrariness:

> For me you took on the enigmatic quality that all tyrants have whose rights are based on their person and not on reason... you, so tremendously the authoritative man, did not keep the commandments you imposed on me. Hence the world was for me divided... one [world] in which I, the slave, lived under laws that had been invented only for me and which I could, I did not know why, never completely comply with; then a second world, which was infinitely remote from mine, in which you lived, concerned with government.... (Kafka 1953, 21, 27)

Adorno and Horkheimer depict authoritarian parental irrationality not as characteristic of an odd family here and there, but as built into the socio-economic structure of the family within certain social orders. While Adorno and Horkheimer focused on paternal attitudes, the aspects of misrecognition to which they refer can equally result from maternal misrecognition. The harsh super-ego they described as a product of paternal authoritarianism may in fact emanate from bad objects produced by pre-Oedipal maternal misrecognition.

Another aspect of misrecognition, highlighted by Alice Miller, concerns mothers' use of their infants as their "narcissistic extensions." Such misrecognition easily reproduces itself as, according to Miller, the abused infant will treat other people, notably its own future children, as narcissistic extensions of itself.[16] One of the most elaborate accounts of maternal misrecognition as the cause of a narcissistic disturbance is Kohut's. According to Kohut, maternal misrecognition amounts to a failure to perform the narcissistic *selfobject* functions of "mirroring," "idealization" and "twinship." This failure prevents a gradual integration

---

16 Alice Miller (1981, 1983) lays special emphasis on the process of the reproduction of narcissistic abuse. The idea that love relations and relations to children are repetitions of relations to our parents is of course familiar. Miller summarizes the causes for reproduction: "1. The unconscious need to pass on to others the humiliation one had undergone oneself; 2. The need to find an outlet for repressed affect; 3. The need to possess and have at one's disposal a vital object to manipulate; 4. Self defense: i.e., the need to idealize one's childhood and one's parents by dogmatically applying the parents' pedagogical principles to one's own children; 5. fear of freedom; 6. Fear of the reappearance of what one has repressed, which one reencounters in one's child and must try to stamp out, having killed it in oneself earlier; 7. revenge for the pain one has suffered." (Miller 1981, 97-98)

of the infant's narcissism with the rest of its personality and results in a fixation on the grandiose "narcissistic self" and the ego ideal (Kohut 1985b).

Each of the aforementioned aspects of maternal misrecognition has its own typical authoritarian consequences. The different accounts of maternal misrecognition are not mutually exclusive but complementary. Winnicott, for example, dwells on an existential experience of emptiness, lack of autonomy and integrity resulting from maternal misrecognition. The account he offers in terms of a somewhat phenomenological Self-psychology can be supplemented by, for example, Klein's account of the object-world produced by maternal misrecognition. The experience of ego weakness and of having one's center outside oneself can be simultaneously understood as reflecting an unindividuated object-world, in Klein's terms, and a false self, in Winnicott's terms. The false self reflects the dominance of a hidden persecutory object while decentering expectations, generative of false selves, reinforce persecutory objects. Object-world integration corresponds to stable, recognized selfhood, both produced within a secure "transitional space."

Authoritarian ideals aim to deny and reverse individuation (Barshack 2000). These ideals are not projections of secure attachments, like many reconciled and alienated ideals, but reflect the grandeur of the persecutory object. They simultaneously license instinctual outlets and impose arbitrary constraints. In the absence of a well-established identity within a differentiated social structure, and as a result of the concomitant preoccupation with power, authoritarian ideals provide particularly aggressive interpretations to standards of recognition, such as, masculinity, respectability and group-membership. As Mosse writes,

> On balance, the ideal of manliness served the right better than the left, by stressing hierarchy as well as equality, pointing the way toward personal and national regeneration, and using evocative pre-industrial symbols... Although the right and the left shared the ideal of respectability, it was the right that pushed it to its limits. The undoubted devotion of the right to the power and strength of the nation served to tighten the alliance between nationalism and respectability... (Mosse 1985, 130)

The authoritarian construction of independent and courageous masculinity may be seen as an attempt to deny or remedy failed individuation-separation. According to Theweleit (1987, 61), authoritarianism attaches value to whatever helps authoritarian men evade the danger they see in women, as misrecognizing mothers. "These men claim to 'love' the very things that *protect* them against real love-object relations": fatherland, nation, uniform, troops, weapons. Theweleit's observation illustrates how authoritarian ideals express primary longings and reflect artificial rather than secure attachments.

Frenkel-Brunswick describes the compensatory, contrived authoritarian persona as,

> ...a stress on virility going hand in hand with an underlying passivity and receptivity which leads to the wish to follow a strong leader... The avoidance of ambiguity and the need for absolutes is but an attempt to counteract the internal chaos and lack of social and personality identity... it is repressed fear of one's own weakness and lack of masculinity which prevents the development of pity for the weak in the ethnocentric... (Frenkel-Brunswick 1954, 264-65)

Authoritarian lack of mature, non-paranoiac identification leads to an inflated presence of mythology as an alternative basis for power. In their accounts of Mussolini and Begin as leaders deeply steeped in fantasy, Silone and Shapiro illustrate the mode of operation of inflated fascist mythology.

> A few years ago some Italian historians were arguing about the period in which the origin of their nation should be set... nobody, not even a fascist historian dared assert that Italian history went back to classical antiquity. This didn't prevent Mussolini from inflating that historical nonsense about Italy's Roman tradition until he had made this the central myth of Fascist ideology. (Silone 1964, 98)

> Herut [Begin's party] was headed by a leader who exercised one-man rule. His strength emanated from his being perceived as the symbol and the embodiment of myths with which party members and voters identified... [Begin's] election by his fellows since 1943 was by acclamation, not by a procedure that enabled real political contest. It was here that the myth of camaraderie was born. The 'fighting family' became an instrument of political order guaranteeing unity and discipline. It was a barrier to any criticism and the ground of the ultimate punishment for any challenge to Begin's leadership – total expulsion or rejection to the periphery. Begin bore the insignia of an exclusive heir, the man who had sat at the feet of the original leader and source of legitimation – Ze'ev Jabotinsky. Those whose political fate depended on the prestige of the leader found protection in this ambience. The leader took supreme responsibility for their deeds, and they, in return for loyalty, were spared punishment. This was a major source of Begin's ineffectiveness in implementing policy, in that he did not have effective control over the actions he authorized. At critical junctions, from *Altelena* affair to the

> war in Lebanon, the same logic was operative: absolute loyalty in return for absolute protection of his followers – even when they were negligent, remiss, or guilty of unbecoming behaviour and moral infractions. (Shapiro 1991, 2, 216)

Having presented a rather general outline of the authoritarian position, the next section will provide a more detailed account of authoritarianism, beginning with some authoritarian characteristics that were convincingly described by the Frankfurt School. In the third section, the complementary Kleinian perspective on authoritarianism will be elaborated. One of the purposes of the following sections is to elaborate on the theoretical psychoanalytic account of authoritarianism by invoking and applying relevant Kleinian concepts.

The Freudian political psychology of the Frankfurt School

Freud regarded the Oedipus complex as the crucial phase in the establishment of mature identification, notably with both parents. In Freudian terms, authoritarianism would be traced to a deficient resolution of the Oedipus complex. This claim is not, in fact, highly contestable, because even if the roots of authoritarianism precede the Oedipus complex, they are still operative in the course of the Oedipus complex and interfere with its 'successful' resolution. Early maternal misrecognition hampers the creation of the conditions for a successful resolution of the Oedipus complex.[17] The Freudian account of the Oedipus complex and its resolution sheds light on the development of the authoritarian personality after its genesis in early maternal misrecognition. One of the deficient patterns of resolution of the Oedipus complex available for the authoritarian personality and described by Freud came to *define* authoritarianism in the eyes of Adorno and Horkheimer:

> The super-ego retains the character of the father, while the more powerful the Oedipus complex was and the more rapidly it succumbed to repression ... the stricter will be the dominance of the super-ego over the ego later on... (Freud 1923a, 34)

---

[17] On the "depressive" conditions for the Oedipus complex see Segal's paper "The Oedipus Complex Today" (1997, 86-95).

In his discussion of the emergence of the ego ideal, Freud himself suggested the relation between inflated super-ego and violent id, both attributed later on to the authoritarian personality.

> The ideal ego is now the target of the self-love which was enjoyed in childhood by the actual ego.... Idealization is possible in the sphere of ego-libido as well as in that of object-libido... It is precisely in neurotics that we find the highest differences of potential between the development of their ego ideal and the amount of sublimation of their primitive libidinal instincts.... (Freud 1914, 94)

Freud suggests that such a personality structure can be traced back to pre-Oedipal ego weakness. Ego weakness implies deficient separation and inability to mitigate and integrate hatred. A cruel and repressive super-ego is introjected as an agent of the id. Another characteristic of the authoritarian personality suggested by Freud (1919) is the sado-masochistic nature of identification with father under heightened anxiety.

The Frankfurt School's groundbreaking account of the authoritarian personality, in particular of authoritarian super-ego, derives from Freud's theory of the super-ego. Freud's group psychology inspired the Frankfurt School's reflections on leadership and the masses. The early work of Erich Fromm, too, inspired the psychological studies of Horkheimer, Adorno and their associates. Each had a different conception of the psychology of authoritarianism, with different emphases. From the beginning, Erich Fromm's work took a separate, controversial path. I shall present his conception of authoritarianism in brief. While Fromm increasingly withdrew from central Freudian conceptions, it would have been artificial to separate his ideas from those of Horkheimer, Adorno and their associates who remained in the Thirties closer to Freud's doctrines.[18] All shared important concepts and political concerns, and Fromm's substantial insights into the nature of authoritarianism can, on the whole, be translated into Freudian terms.

Many of the underlying ideas of *The Authoritarian Personality* are already present in Fromm's early articles and in his study on *The Working Class in Weimar Germany* (1984), conducted and written in the Thirties,

---

[18] Adorno criticized, for example, Fromm's attempts to reconcile civilization and libido. Only a recognition of the tension between the two can serve, according to Adorno, as a basis for social criticism.

and earlier still, in Reich's analysis of fascism.[19] In his working-class study, Fromm's main intention was to examine the correlation between Marxist and democratic commitments. He defined individuals who exhibited both commitments as "reliable anti-Nazis." Fromm perceived authoritarianism as a longing for domination and a worship of power.

> The authoritarian attitude affirms, seeks out and enjoys the subjugation of men under a higher external power, whether this power is the state or a leader, natural law, the past or God... The strong and powerful are simply admired and loved for these qualities, the weak and helpless hated and despised. Sacrifice and duty, and not pleasure in life and happiness, are the guiding aims of the authoritarian attitude. (1984, 209-10)

This conception continued to underlie Fromm's studies in political psychology, such as, *Escape from Freedom* and *The Analysis of Human Destructiveness.* Fromm's working-class study, anticipating *The Authoritarian Personality*, is also marked by the variety of activities examined in relation to political conviction: cultural and intellectual pursuits, habits, social life and so on. Fromm continued to articulate his conception of authoritarianism in *Escape from Freedom.* There, he convincingly lays emphasis, as in his early articles dating from the early Thirties, on the relevance of the psychoanalytic understanding of sado-masochism to the analysis of authoritarianism. Authoritarianism is defined as a sado-masochistic "striving for submission and domination" that expresses a striving for symbiotic unity intended "to acquire the strength which the individual self is lacking" (1941, 141). "Both the masochistic and sadistic strivings tend to help the individual to escape his unbearable feeling of aloneness and powerlessness." (1941, 151) "[The sado-masochistic person] admires authority and tends to submit to it, but at the same time he wants to be an authority himself and have others submit to him." (1941, 163) Fromm distinguishes between sadism and

---

[19] Fromm's articles from the early Thirties already analyzed authoritarianism from the perspective of the psychoanalytic theory of sado-masochism. Among the essays included in Fromm's *The Crisis of Psychoanalysis: Essays on Freud, Marx and Social Psychology* (1970), see "The Method and Function of an analytical social psychology" (135-62) and "Psychoanalytic characterology and its relevance for social psychology" (163-89), both originally published in 1932. On Fromm's Weimar's study see Brunner (1994). Essays by Wilhelm Reich on political psychology from the same period are collected in *Sex-Pol Essays 1929-1934* (1972). Reich's major analysis of fascism – *The Mass Psychology of Fascism* – first appeared in 1933.

destructiveness. While the sadistic person is dependent on his object and does not wish to destroy it, the destructive character is more narcissistic and strives to destroy whatever he encounters (Fromm 1975, 387).[20]

For Fromm, authoritarianism, destructiveness and sado-masochism are understood in terms of a desperate striving for symbiosis, even at the price of punishment and misery. The "feeling of certainty and identity depends on this symbiosis; to be rejected by the authority means to be thrown into a void, to face the horror of nothingness." (Fromm 1947, 151) Symbiosis is sought after both by sadistic and masochistic characters because "neither has his center in himself" (Fromm 1975, 26). Fromm's account is remarkably similar to Winnicott's conception of the false self as a product of excessive discipline and constraint. The self is transplanted outside, in the fulfillment of external expectations.

> When the parents, acting as agents of society, start to suppress the child's spontaneity and independence, the growing child feels more and more unable to stand on its own feet; it therefore seeks for the magic helper and often makes the parents the personification of 'him'. (Fromm 1941, 178)

> The scars left from the child's defeat in the fight against irrational authority are to be found at the bottom of every neurosis. They form a syndrome the most important features of which are the weakening or paralysis of the person's originality and spontaneity; the weakening of the self and the substitution of a pseudo self in which the feeling of 'I am' is dulled and replaced by the experience of self as the sum total of others' expectations... (Fromm 1947, 161)

Here, Fromm is more specific about the results of parental authoritarian attitudes than Horkheimer and the authors of *The Authoritarian Personality*. Horkheimer, for example, offers only vague suggestions regarding the precise psychological mechanisms set in motion by the experience of irrational paternal authority.

Alongside the studies of Fromm, Horkheimer's work in the Thirties served as the main source of inspiration for *The Authoritarian Personality*. The focus of Horkheimer's interest lay in the crisis of paternal authority following the transformation of the economic structure of the family and in the political consequences of this crisis. Both Fromm and Horkheimer generally kept to their early formulations on the nature

---

[20] *See* Theweleit (1989, 216-18) on fascism as anti-production.

of authoritarianism. Their early interest in political psychology was directly related to Marxist motivations, but gradually authoritarianism and anti-Semitism became phenomena worthy of being investigated independently of concrete political programs and affiliations. To convey the gist of Horkheimer's position, I shall quote at length from some of his essays that range from a long period of work.

According to Horkheimer, the decline of the bourgeois family and its economic rationales undermined traditional paternal authority. "Authority in the home assumes an irrational aspect" (Horkheimer 1949, 361) due to the decline of the socio-economic role of the family. Paternal authority, once rendered irrational, becomes weaker and more repressive. "The more the family as an essential economic unit loses ground in Western civilization, the more society emphasizes its conventional forms..." (Horkheimer 1949, 362) Furthermore, there emerges a contradiction in modern society between the roles family members play and their self-conception as "abstract subjects of self-interest" (Horkheimer 1949, 365).

> Because of this separation in space and time between professional and familial life, every bourgeois father may in social life have a very modest position and have to bend the knee to others, yet at home he will be the master and exercise the highly important function of accustoming his children to discretion and obedience. (Horkheimer 1972, 108)

In the traditional bourgeois family, discipline was not imposed for its own sake and naked power was not admired as such. Harsh discipline may have been "a productive trait... as long as the fate of the individual and the common good both depended, at least in part, on the efficiency of the individual" (Horkheimer 1972, 109).

> At the beginning of the bourgeois age the father's control of his household was doubtless an indispensable condition of progress. The self-control of the individual, the disposition for work and discipline, the ability to hold firmly to certain ideas, consistency in practical life, application of reason, perseverance and pleasure in constructive activity could all be developed, in the circumstances, only under the dictation and guidance of the father whose own education had been won in the school of life. (Horkheimer 1972, 101)

Deprived of its traditional spirit and role, yet still authoritative, the family becomes a mere exercise in obedience (Horkheimer 1949, 365). Horkheimer concludes that,

> [w]hereas the authoritarian or sado-masochistic character is by no means

> a novel phenomenon and can be observed throughout the history of middle-class society, it is its peculiar abstractness and callousness which seem to be symptomatic of a world which adheres to familial authority after the inner substance of the family has been dissolved... (Horkheimer 1949, 369)

The decline of paternal authority results in a general crisis of moral autonomy.[21] Children can no longer establish mature identification with paternal authority and remain in immediate need of powerful external authorities, such as, leaders and groups. The child's discovery that the parents' authoritative attitude was a mere façade propels a quest for an unfailingly strong authority and an eager endorsement of any authority that put itself forward (Horkheimer 1949, 365).

> The father as an arbitrary power no longer offers possibilities of identification, and the child instead identifies with repressive social instances. (Horkheimer 1972, 127)

> The son identifies himself with groups who exercise strength through numerical superiority, rather than with one single clear-cut person setting an 'ego-ideal' to the young. What is affected is not so much belief in authority *per se*, which in a way is stronger today than it used to be during the last century, but the formation of an integrated, continuously functioning super-ego. The consistent ego and super-ego, the essential traits of the traditional middle class idea of the individual, are necessarily undermined in modern society. (Horkheimer 1950, 217)

Paternal authoritarianism is often accompanied by a similar attitude on the mother's part.[22] Mothers reproduce paternal authoritarian attitudes and the repressive economic and emotional patterns of authoritarian society. "Because the woman bows to the laws of the patriarchal family, she becomes an instrument for maintaining authority in this society." (Horkheimer 1972, 121) Furthermore, "it is not only in this direct way… that the woman exercises the function of strengthening authority. Her whole position in the family results in an inhibiting of important psychic energies which might have been effective in shaping the world...." (Horkheimer 1972, 120-21). In Kleinian terms, the object-world created by authoritarian mothering – one that is ruled by internalized

---

[21] On the decline of paternal authority see also Mitscherlich (1969) and Marcuse, "The Obsolescence of the Freudian concept of Man" in *Five Lectures* (1970). On Lacan's early conception of paternal authority see Dews (1995).

[22] *See* Rumpf (1993).

misrecognition (misrecognizing objects) – predisposes the child to authoritarianism. While maternal love used to be the source of the individual's capacity for care, pity – "that very same quality which used to reflect more than anything else the mother's love for her child" (Horkheimer 1949, 369) – and for utopian aspirations for a better world, it now no longer functions as a shelter from the hostility of the external world. Horkheimer observes in the "authoritarian child of our times" a combination of ego weakness and toughness.

> He represses the child in himself... and behaves as a scheming little adult with no consistent independent ego but with a tremendous amount of narcissism. His being hard-boiled and at the same time submissive in the face of real power predisposes him for totalitarian forms of life... Toughness, ruthlessness, and the forced display of masculinity, all leading to politico-fascist ideologies, are generally linked with a disturbed relationship toward the mother or, perhaps even more, with the lack of any genuine relationship with her. (Horkheimer 1949, 367, 370)

If totalitarianism results from the demise of the traditional family (a family like Horkheimer's own), then the latter must be restored to overcome authoritarianism and authoritarian mass culture. The traditional family, Horkheimer argued, offered its members a wealth of meaningful practices within the private sphere.

> The same economic changes which destroy the family bring about the danger of totalitarianism... family in crisis produces the attitudes which predispose men for blind submission... the modern family in fact produces the ideal objects of totalitarian integration... (Horkheimer 1949, 365)

> ...the family was a place where suffering could be given free expression and the injured individual found a retreat within which he or she could put up some resistance. In the economy people were being reduced to mere functions of one or another economic factor: wealth or technically demanding physical or mental work. The same process of reduction to sub-personal status was going on within the family insofar as the father was becoming the money-earner, the woman a sexual object or a domestic servant... Within the family, however, unlike public life, relationships were not mediated through the market and the individual members were not competing with each other. Consequently the individual always had the possibility there of living not as a mere function but as a human being... In civic life, even when common concerns... had an essentially negative character... common concerns took a positive form in sexual love and especially in maternal care. The growth

> and happiness of the other are willed in such unions. A felt opposition therefore arises between them and hostile reality outside. To this extent, the family does not only educate for authority in bourgeois society; it also cultivates the dream of a better condition for mankind. In the yearning of many adults for the paradise of their childhood, in the way a mother can speak of her son even though he has come into conflict with the world, in the protective love of a wife for her husband, there are ideas and forces at work which admittedly are not dependent on the existence of the family in its present form, and, in fact, are even in danger of shriveling up in such a milieu, but which, nevertheless, in the bourgeois system of life, rarely have any place but the family where they can survive at all. (Horkheimer 1972, 114-15)

Adorno, Fromm and Winnicott held a similar view of the democratic potential of the traditional family.[23] The force of rational, as opposed to charismatic, authority derives from the strength of the private sphere. In contrast to these views, Reich sometimes seems to consider the family as inevitably authoritarian. “In the figure of the father the authoritarian state has its representative in the family, so that the family becomes its most important instrument of power.” (Reich 1970, 53) Horkheimer was fascinated by Hegel's view of the family and under Hegel’s influence conceived of the family as a separate sphere, opposed to society at large and identified with the maternal. Horkheimer is right to recognize the ethical necessity of firm attachments within the ‘traditional’ family and their far-reaching progressive implications. Nevertheless, he still focuses on the crisis of paternal authority and super-ego in a way that confuses authoritarianism with alienated liberalism, both being products of

---

[23] According to Adorno, "[w]ith the family there passes away, while the system lasts, not only the most effective agency of the bourgeoisie, but also the resistance which, though repressing the individual, also strengthened, perhaps even produced him. The end of the family paralyzes the forces of opposition. The rising collectivist order is a mockery of a classless one: together with the bourgeois it liquidates the utopia that once drew sustenance from motherly love." (Adorno 1974, 23) On the relation between the decline of the family and the rise of fascism see also Fromm (1941, 215). On Nazism's war against the family see also Theweleit (1989, 252). According to Winnicott (1965), "[t]here is special significance in the devotion of the ordinary good mother to her infant, the capacity for eventual emotional maturity being founded as a result of the devotion. Mass interference at this point, in a society, would quickly and effectualy lessen the democratic potential of that society, just as it would diminish the richness of its culture."

misrecognition. In his moral and political psychology, Winnicott comes closer than Horkheimer to an understanding of the ethical significance of maternal recognition. This is a widespread criticism of Horkheimer (Benjamin 1977b, 127). It was more likely the decline of the maternal rather than paternal principle, following economic and sociological transformations, which prompted the eruption of fascism and authoritarianism. A focus on ego weakness rather than on the rigidity of the super-ego would have given the maternal influence its due recognition. While from a Kleinian perspective, a weak ego would be naturally accompanied by a persecutory super-ego, from a Freudian perspective there is no such obvious relation, to the effect that the Frankfurt School account of authoritarianism remains incomplete. The Frankfurt School account inherited some of the general flaws of the Freudian conception of the Oedipal paternal super-ego as the exclusive basis of morality.

The Frankfurt School's focus on paternal authoritarianism is not only exaggerated, but its very conception of ideal paternal authority, paternal rationality and the traditional patriarchal family is confused. Adorno and Horkheimer neither carefully distinguish nor link the different aspects and conditions of the rationality for which they are nostalgic. Rationality is alternately said to be conditioned by labor, opposition to nature, a certain social relation (perhaps alienation) and a certain economic structure. Self-interest, too, plays a part in the complex conditions of lost rationality and so does morality, as opposed to formal, legalist and economic reason. In addition to these conditions for rationality, there are the various conditions that have to be secured within the family, such as, fairness and consistency.[24]

The Authoritarian Personality

Fromm and Horkheimer launched the Frankfurt School's occupation with authoritarianism and described authoritarian character traits which were to be systematically compiled in *The Authoritarian Personality*. Let us now take a closer look at some of these characteristics. The authoritarian personality, according to the 'F-scale' (the scale measuring fascist inclinations), can be identified by nine main characteristics

---

[24] On Adorno's and Horkheimer's different conceptions of reason, see Benjamin (1977b).

(Adorno *et al.* 1950, 228): (a) conventionalism; (b) authoritarian submission; (c) authoritarian aggression; (d) anti-intraception; (e) superstition and stereotypy; (f) power and "toughness;" (g) destructiveness and cynicism; (h) projectivity (defined as "[t]he disposition to believe that wild and dangerous things go on in the world; the projection outwards of unconscious emotional impulses."); (i) "exaggerated concern with sexual 'goings-on'."

In the following discussion, I will not follow closely this list of characteristics but focus on some fundamental ones. According to Adorno, Horkheimer and their associates, the authoritarian personality is marked by a *weak ego*, a *strong* and *violent id* and a *harsh* and *stern super-ego* – all resulting from an authoritarian object of identification (Adorno *et al.* 1950, 456, 595; Horkheimer 1950). The authoritarian personality lacks integration and resorts to excessive repression (Frenkel-Brunswick 1954, 265). After considering personality *disintegration* we shall move on to consider *fusion.* Fusion with the leader and the group is said to express authoritarian ego weakness. According to Fromm, fusion functions as an escape from meaninglessness. The authoritarian personality forms symbiotic, sado-masochistic domination-oriented relationships. Finally, authoritarian *conformity* will be discussed. The emptiness of the authoritarian ego, its dependence upon external confirmation and its violence lead to conformity and pseudoconservatism.

Personality Disintegration

According to the Frankfurt School, the authoritarian personality is formed under the influence of paternal authoritarianism that weakens the ego and produces a stern and exacting super-ego, a "strict, conventional super ego to which there is a complete surrender" (Frenkel-Brunswick and Sanford 1946, 117). Adorno explains that the authoritarian personality emerges from a sado-masochistic resolution of the Oedipus complex, a strict repression of emotion and a phony transformation of hatred of the father into love (Adorno *et al.* 1950, 751). The resulting, excessively rigid super-ego is an externalized, rather than internalized, authority (Adorno *et al.* 1950, 754-62).

Adorno and Horkheimer were misguided in focusing almost exclusively on the crisis of paternal authority and paternal super-ego as the source of authoritarianism. Moreover, Adorno and Horkheimer failed to emphasize adequately the differences between authoritarian and 'successful' resolutions of the Oedipus complex and to distinguish between their respective advantages and disadvantages. Many aspects of the regression ascribed by the Frankfurt School to the authoritarian super-ego actually form part of any normal resolution of the Oedipus complex.[25] While Adorno and Horkheimer initially tried to draw a distinction between authoritarian and non-authoritarian super-ego, their criticisms of the former can be leveled against the latter, as well. Classical psychoanalytic theory expects every resolution of the Oedipus complex to involve repression – for example, of hatred towards parents – and various other regressive phenomena, such as, identification with the aggressor, denial of aggression and idealization of parents. The conspicuous regressive aspect of the Oedipus complex partly explains the oscillation in Frankfurt School texts between condemnations of the modern social order *en bloc* and of authoritarianism in particular.[26] Only later on did Adorno explicitly criticize the psychoanalytic ideal of Oedipal normality for the regressions it allows. Adorno criticized the Freudian idealization of the super-ego and the whole ideal of an integrated personality in a society that institutionalizes contradiction and exploitation. Adorno (1968, 82) posited that the super-ego is the representative of social conventions, hampering the ego's emancipatory efforts. This criticism of the super-ego was implicitly present from the start. It was at first leveled only against the harsh authoritarian super-ego, while it was always applicable in principle also to the 'normal' Freudian super-ego.

It was Klein who understood the broad ethical implications of 'successful' resolutions of the Oedipus complex as assuming and facilitating non-paranoiac object relations based on the predominance of good and trustworthy objects. Horkheimer and Adorno do observe the greater autonomy and self-sufficiency of a non-authoritarian super-ego. However, it may be argued that it is the essentially authoritarian regression involved in the Oedipus complex that contributes to these

---

[25] Deleuze and Guattari (1983) draw politically radical conclusions from the paranoid regressions they take to be involved in the 'successful' resolution of the Oedipus complex.

[26] In a series of writings, Deleuze and Guattari provide a thorough critique of modern bourgeois society based on the regressive nature of the supposed resolution of the Oedipus complex.

ethically positive effects. The self-constraint, future autonomy and relative integration of the ideal Oedipus may all derive from compromise with the id, leveling of individuality and identification with the aggressor. The tracing of authoritarianism to an authoritarian father is problematic also in that it may generate confusion between the authoritarian and alienated positions, because paternal authoritarianism produces alienated liberalism (when there is no shortage of recognition in the private sphere).

Symbiotic Identification with 'Persecutory Objects'

The craving for symbiosis with omnipotent objects is one of the important features of the authoritarian personality and it has been given various theoretical formulations. This aspect of ego weakness was most thoroughly discussed by Fromm. Many of its various manifestations are also discussed in *The Authoritarian Personality*. Freud stated that in love and narcissistic identification other persons occupy the place of one's ego or super-ego, and that in cases of ego weakness, these symbiotic processes become excessive. In *The Ego and the Id,* Freud suggests a notion of ego strength as the ability to resist such excess in identification.[27] A Kleinian interpretation of the authoritarian craving for symbiosis will be discussed in the following section. Klein's conception of the allure of the schizoid-paranoid position readily accounts for the authoritarian drift towards symbiosis.

Symbiotic identification involves excessive idealization and admiration, processes observed in the authoritarian personality's relation to its self-image,[28] family, nation, leader, and the world. Fromm notes a striving for symbiosis with the existing world-order, as a whole: "Fate

---

[27] Jung refers to symbiotic identifications as instances of "psychic inflation" (1966, 143). According to Odajnyk's reconstruction of Jung's view, psychic inflation involves a vicious circle: "...identification is attractive because it 'offers easy compensation for personal deficiencies.' But, on the other hand, the identification does not allow for the development of the personality, and therefore increases the sense of personal deficiency, which, in turn, strengthens the identification with the compensating transpersonal elements." (Odajnyk 1976, 20) Odajnyk quotes Jung (1966, 145).

[28] On idealized self-conception, see *The Authoritarian Personality* (Adorno *et al.* 1950, 430), Klein (1952, 73) and Kohut (1971).

may be rationalized philosophically as 'natural law' or as 'destiny of man', religiously as the 'will of the Lord', ethically as 'duty' – for the authoritarian character it is always a higher power outside of the individual, toward which the individual can do nothing but submit." (Fromm 1941, 170) Adorno detects the same striving behind the preoccupation with astrology. Astrology reflects a striving for loss of freedom and for external determination of one's fate which results in acceptance of the existing order, the status quo (Adorno 1994, 116,121).[29] Authoritarian idealization of one's *kin group* has been thoroughly noted and studied.

> The findings have shown that subjects who may be regarded as highly susceptible to fascist propaganda profess an ideology calling for rigid, uncritical identification with the family and reveal their absolute submission to familial authority in early infancy... The fascist-minded people in the study almost invariably idealized their parents. A typical interviewee answered the question as to whom he regarded as the greatest personalities in history: my parents. This cult of the parents is in most cases based on the adoration of a stern and punitive father. (Horkheimer 1949, 368) [30]

A feigned national unity of all individuals, of parents and children (unity of generations), is ceaselessly celebrated. "[T]he masses... try to escape their own despair, taking refuge behind the emblems of a distant age in which all social contradictions are 'symbolically' resolved, men are 'symbolically' brothers, and capitalist profits are 'symbolically' eliminated." (Silone 1964, 91)[31] Since authoritarian children cannot admit or express any hostility towards their parents, their repressed hostility accumulates (Horkheimer 1949, 368; Frenkel-Brunswick 1954, 234, 264-65).[32] This hostility is often displaced onto weak racial or political minorities (Fromm 1941, 211).

---

[29] On fascism and fate see also Frenkel-Brunswick and Sanford (1946, 96-124).

[30] See also Frenkel-Brunswick's rich paper (1954, 240) and Miller (1981, ch. 3) on adults' repression of their being derided and exploited as children. Fromm already studied idealization of parents in his Weimar study (1984). On "image of parents" see also *The Authoritarian Personality* (Adorno *et al.* 1950, 359-66).

[31] On feigned unity see also Adorno (1978, 131).

[32] Kogan (1956) supports the correspondence between authoritarian personality, repression of weaknesses and repressed hatred of parents. On repression as the main root of fascism see Reich (1970).

> [R]esistance against paternal authority is displaced and turned exclusively against the weak, the underdog. Accordingly, family acceptance serves to express the subject's social narcissism. The parents, the siblings, and the whole in-group are always 'wonderful people'; the others are 'not on the level', slovenly, lowly. (Horkheimer 1949, 368)

Some of the functions performed by the figure of the idealized parent are taken up by the authoritarian leader. Frankfurt School studies illuminated mechanisms that structure the operation of fascist leadership. Freud's study of group psychology and regressive social behavior served as a theoretical bedrock, for example, for Adorno's paper "Freudian Theory and the Pattern of Fascist Propaganda" (1978). Adorno assumes that the narcissistic identification of the authoritarian personality with the leader involves idealizations of the group, as a whole, and of its leadership. Adorno does not specify in this article in what sense identification is narcissistic. According to Freud (1914, 1921, 1923a), every identification involves narcissistic desexualization of its object, and it is widely accepted that mature psychic life involves a 'healthy' narcissistic dimension expressed, for example, in ideals and group attachments. Idealized self-images embodied in a leader-figure are not, as such, particularly regressive. Except for his observation that the authoritarian personality often finds in its leader its exact mirror-reflection, Adorno does not to specify the regressive tinge of authoritarian identification by merely calling it narcissistic. The identifications to which Adorno refers are regressive because they are symbiotic and 'primary'. 'Primary identification' is, according to Freud, indeed symbiotic, and, in the Kleinian tradition, narcissism is understood as regression to the primary schizoid-paranoid symbiotic position. Adorno does clearly identify another regressive aspect of the authoritarian personality's relation to its leader, namely, the sado-masochistic aspect.

> The formation of the imagery of an omnipotent and unbridled father figure, by far transcending the individual father and therewith apt to be enlarged into a 'group ego' is the only way to promulgate the passive-masochistic attitude... to whom one's will has to be surrendered. (Adorno 1978, 124)

Adorno shows how in order to encourage identification, fascist leaders instinctively strive to appear as ordinary people. At the same time, they have to be conceived of as thoroughly self-indulgent. "[T]he leader can be loved only if he himself does not love..." (Adorno 1978,

127).[33] The masochist authoritarian crowd worships a leader who takes no interest in it. Hitler created an image of a leader indifferent to everyday concerns of government[34] and one believing that if his people is defeated on the battlefield it deserves ruin. “What matters if England is the hammer and we the anvil, so long as violence reigns and not servile Christian timidity?” asks the narrator in Borges’s “Deutsches Requiem”. Contrary to appearances, extreme national self-assertiveness is a form of self-destructiveness. As it has often been suggested, the authoritarian mass supports the leader contrary to its own interests.[35] Its love for the leader is self-destructive. Self-destructiveness excludes the possibility of rational politics, namely, politics that is aimed towards some ‘common good’, such as, justice, tradition, utility, or, at the very least, peace. If the aggression harbored by the Hobbesian man can be checked by the fabrication of an intimidating sovereign thanks to man’s self-preserving rationality, such rationality is powerless in the face of self-destructiveness. The solidarity between fascist parties of different – potentially conflicting – countries is revealing. It amounts to a general affirmation of the prospects of war, extinction and self-extinction. The idea that fascist masses vote contrary to their own interests lends itself to a conceptual debate. Sometimes this idea is plainly incorrect: sheer fascist destructiveness may be advantageous to somebody's personal interests. However, when fascism threatens the interests of the fascist crowd, the latter is normally not manipulated into believing the contrary by means of rhetorical tricks. The crowd acts contrary to its own interests because it desires self-destruction.[36]

---

[33] On the ordinary man image of fascist leader see *The Dialectic of Enlightenment* (Adorno and Horkheimer 1986, 236).

[34] "Hitler tried to project an image of being above the fray, aloof and uninvolved in governmental dross, but somehow all powerful and talking to the nation in a *mise-en-scène* conceived for a pagan deity." (Lewin 1997, 120)

[35] "...sexual inhibition changes the structure of economically suppressed man in such a way that he acts, feels, and thinks contrary to his own material interests." (Reich 1970, 32)

[36] "... the fundamental problem of political philosophy is still precisely the one that Spinoza saw so clearly, and that Wilhelm Reich rediscovered: ‘Why do men fight *for* their servitude as stubbornly as though it were their salvation?’... Reich is at his profoundest as a thinker when he refuses to accept ignorance or illusion on the part of the masses as an explanation of fascism, and demands an

The sado-masochistic relation of a mass to its leader has been highlighted by the Frankfurt School since their early preoccupation with authoritarianism. According to Adorno, "[t]he unconscious psychological desire for self-annihilation faithfully reproduces the structure of a political movement which ultimately transforms its followers into victims" (1946, 137). In *Authority and the Family* (1972, 110), Horkheimer speaks of the tendency to "surrender their will to some sort of leader". Later, he describes the performance of the leader in the fascist ritual:

> He conveys the notion that the individual is nothing and that the mass of individuals is equally nothing. All they can do is to attempt to survive, and they must hurry to surrender their own nothingness to the stronger ones. For the nation is threatened by evil forces. Only by complete submission to the leader and by complete identification with his crusade can the individual and the nation be saved.... The speech is a foretaste of the great crusade and the destruction it will wreak. (Horkheimer 1950, 233)

From his very early writings onwards, Fromm considered sado-masochism, including sado-masochistic relation to the leader, as definitive of authoritarianism. In *The Anatomy of Human Destructiveness*, he analyzes Hitler's conspicuous indifference to the suffering of the Germans (Fromm 1975, 479). Fromm understands masochism in the present context as "aiming at dissolving oneself in an overwhelmingly strong power and participating in its strength and glory" (Fromm 1941, 221, 232). In his essay on "The Psychology of Quislingism" (1951), Jones analyzes the authoritarian personality's admiration of the strong and the aggressive: aggression is conceived by the authoritarian personality as sexual potency. According to Jones, the fascist is an insecure or dissatisfied person who idealizes his father. In

---

explanation that will take their desires into account, an explanation formulated in terms of desire: no, the masses were not innocent dupes; at a certain point, under a certain set of conditions, they *wanted* fascism, and it is this perversion of desire of the masses that needs to be accounted for." (Deleuze and Guattari 1983, 29) Deleuze and Guattari explain the fight for servitude by invoking the role of repression and anti-production in the dynamics of capitalism. On the issue of political action against one's interests see also Adorno (1967, 80) and Zizek (1991). See also the chapter in Machiavelli's *Discourses* entitled "On how the populace often seeks its own ruin, taken by some plan with a misleading appearance of being in its interests" (Machiavelli 1994, 144).

turn, this idealization establishes a sado-masochistic relation to authority.

Even if these descriptions are generally correct, they need to be couched in a wider context. The sado-masochistic relation to the leader and to the group forms part of a general regression to the sado-masochistic order of *communitas*, in which the functioning of leadership changes in several ways. Since social roles evaporate in *communitas*, the leader can no longer occupy a structural *role* of leadership.[37] The relation between the authoritarian leader and his following is immediate, that is, not mediated by party, administrative apparatus or any other branch of structure (Lewin 1997, 120).[38] In many ways, the leader's authority is of the kind Weber termed 'charismatic.' The fascist leader operates as a private person. His authority is hardly stable and enduring, since he is at once the object of intense love and hate. When such truly popular leaders die, many are in fact relieved because charismatic leaders represent anti-structure. In Israel, Itzhak Rabin stood for structure and his assassination was experienced as the utter, devastating collapse of the entire normative system of roles and meanings. Benjamin Netanyahu, by contrast, was a charismatic leader who enacted strong anti-structural forces. Rabin, like any other rational-traditional authority, ruled in the name of a transcendent corporate personality that is at once benevolent and exacting. Netanyahu's rule was, in the most profound sense, lawless, because it derived its legitimacy from the group as a complete, undivided, immanent entity free from superimposed constraints. Freud's observation that the sudden disintegration of leadership stirs panic equivalent to the terror of an approaching natural disaster should be qualified: it is more evident in the case of leaders who represent structure than in the case of charismatic leaders. The charismatic leader is in danger: the love he stirs may turn into hatred. Indeed, ritual murder of the king, or of other high political and religious authorities, was a widespread phenomenon, which still

---

[37] Shapiro's analysis of the *Likud*'s road to power illustrates how Begin's leadership lacked a structural anchor. "Neither wings of the party worked to construct an institutional structure of any real substance. No organizational apparatus worthy of the name was established..." (Shapiro 1991, 38)

[38] Bataille (1997) wrongly depicts the fascist leader as the transcendent Other of religion. The fascist leader is an immanent, immediately present, divine King-Thing. Bataille draws another wrong analogy between the fascist leader and an army officer: the army officer is located within structure, the fascist leader – outside it.

puzzles anthropological theory.[39] Murder is only a natural consequence of fascist political ritual, such ritual being the pure and climatic enactment of deviant, sado-masochistic *communitas*.

> The performance of the ritual as such functions to a very large extent as the ultimate content of fascist propaganda... some speculation may be allowed with regard to the specific symbolic meaning of the fascist ritual. It is not wide off the mark to interpret it as the offering of a sacrifice. (Adorno 1946, 136)

The fascist leader is sacrificed because his ritual immediacy and Thingness amount to an affirmation of death. While death is ordinarily tamed by being kept in a transcendent distant realm, in ritual the leader enacts the big Other, the M-Other, the source of life and death. In the divine king the mundane and the transcendent are fused. All participants in ritual identify with death[40] and enact the persecutory maternal imago. It is the primary persecutory imago – blending omnipotence, death, symbiosis – that is enacted in rituals. Temporarily, all participants are fearless of death, sharing its timelessness. Death is not timeless because it is the fate of all human beings but because it marks the exit from the order of time, the passage from structure to *communitas*. Participants in ritual are transformed into total Things as their separation-individuation is suspended. In the course of quotidian life, the subject, by being an organ of a timeless structure, indirectly appropriates structure's omnipotence by identifying itself with its central politico-religious spectacle of power. In the fascist ritual, the subject demands and achieves more than that: unlimited, immediate omnipotence and timelessness.

---

[39] Freud (1912-1913) and Girard (1977, 1986, 1987), following Frazer, developed different theories of the ritual murder of priests and kings. There are numerous other writings on this subject, including Frankfort (1948) on the Egyptian festival of the Sed, Burkert (1983) and Alford (1996) on the sacrificial leader.

[40] All rituals involve a transitional celebration of death. Death is affirmed not simply because there is a general reversal of oppositions, as Leach (1976) suggests, or because aggression is less inhibited and sacrifice offered, or because a certain phase of life has just come to an end. Death is celebrated following the breakdown of transcendence and the overwhelming advent of the archaic persecutory maternal imago in ritual narcissism. Then, death can no longer be projected. The transcendent structure of desire collapses, and omnipotence, self-sufficiency and timelessness are appropriated.

The awesome leader who plays the Absolute Other – the envied mother – claims divinity for himself and thereby undermines structure. Undivided into private and public bodies,[41] the fascist leader is outside structure as a system of normative divisions. Whereas ordinary men are infected with Thingness only when they die, the divine king and the fascist leader are sacred Things during their lifetime. They are slaughtered because of the dangerous lethal excess involved in their sacred Thingness. The King-Thing inspires the total, simultaneous love and cruelty characteristic of the symbiotic bond.[42] In his analysis of sacred kingship, Luc de Heusch (1987) links ritual murder to magical kingship, that is, to the king's Thingness. De Heusch distinguishes between two paradigms of leadership: magical leadership, whose authority rests on heroic exploit – such as, slaughter of the predecessor – and leadership whose authority derives from succession. The former corresponds to *communitas*, the latter – to structure. Under magical kingship, exemplified by a fascist régime, the relation between leader and group is modeled on a sado-masochistic symbiosis. According to Anzieu (1984), the charismatic leader in such groups is identified on the fantasy level with the persecuting maternal imago, the imaginary source of death. Where authority rests on succession, the leader guarantees of separation and of the transcendence of the Thing. Anzieu suggests that, like the charismatic leader, his group is also self-generated, forming – together with the leader – a symbiotic, self-sufficient, a-historical and autoerotic whole.

In the political ritual, the authoritarian leader enacts death, the Absolute Master. Images of random shootings in mass rallies in Saddam Hussein's Baghdad provide tangible illustrations of destructive and self-destructive ritual outbursts. The fascist leader may play the forgiving, kind, loving, protective and just father, or stage an offended enraged god. In either case, his words and resolutions descend from heaven, theatrically, slowly, keeping all in suspense. He confirms his absolute power by staging before his anxious audience dramas of cruelty or

---

[41] The widespread application of Kantorowicz's thesis of the king's two bodies to divine kingship (for example, by Schnepel 1991) is misplaced precisely because the divine, magical king is a Thing, undivided into private and public bodies.

[42] According to Lefort (1986), the 'logic of authoritarianism' is indeed the logic of identity of leader and people.

opulent goodness.[43] His decision-making in these dramas appears as super-human and machine-like.[44]

Social solidarity and cohesion depend on leadership in both *communitas* and structure. Theweleit asks: "How then does the Führer function in this system? He seems to represent a link connecting the sons to the domain of the abstract father's power. Since the Führer has access to the father's domain, he knows and executes his will..." (Theweleit 1989, 373). Here, in fact, Theweleit describes the universal role of leaders rather than any peculiarity of the Führer. What does distinguish fascist leadership is its sado-masochistic basis and the absence of structural mediation between leader and group and between the leader and himself. Where a firm structure exists and commands rigid individuation-separation in the form of a network of differentiated, concrete, normative identities, the leader's position is placed within this frame.

The contributors to Ionescu and Gellner's *Populism* (1969) speak of the leader's immediate, direct presence in populist movements. Kershaw (1997) perceptively describes the logic and motivation underlying the entire Nazi régime and industry as that of "working towards the Führer". The Führer's presence is immediate and symbiotic, a revelation of the divine. He is the collective goal in itself, a self-referring "symbolic equation," a unity of signifier and signified.[45] He is neither bound by the hegemonic norms of representation nor by any reality principle. Whatever he says cannot, therefore, be anything but meaningless blubber, were an effort to speak rationally ever made. Of course, the appearance of structure exists in authoritarian régimes with their omnipotent and ramified bureaucracies. Fascist bureaucracy preoccupies itself with discipline and becomes rigidly hierarchical precisely because it maintains

---

[43] See Lewin (1997, 122) on Stalin's and Hitler's penchant for affected and pompous scenes of kindness and cruelty.

[44] On kingship as a machine see Apostolides (1981). Apostolides suggests in passing an account of the disintegration of structural leadership. The preservation of structural leadership depends on the maintenance of a right balance between the King's private and public bodies (154). Apostolides writes also on the imaginary identification of the leader with the persecutory maternal imago.

[45] Some readers may object to such a juxtaposition of Kleinian and Lacanian concepts, but my aim is merely to articulate a political conclusion which stems from both forms of analysis.

structure artificially. It is a pseudo-structure. In authoritarian bureaucracies, organs refuse the burdens of individuality, disappear into their roles and play them sado-masochistically. Contrary to what Adorno implies (1950, 413; 1978, 128), hierarchy in itself is not an authoritarian characteristic. It is present in every structure and is only accentuated under authoritarianism where it becomes one-dimensional and an end in itself.

Conformity

The authors of *The Authoritarian Personality* found that many authoritarian interviewees were violent and rebellious as children and later became obedient and conformist. "The typical prejudiced child, however, appears to make much less of an attempt to manage his own impulses and appears to vacillate between a fearful surface submission to authorities and a comparative neglect of social standards." (Frenkel-Brunswick 1954, 243)[46] Authoritarian destructiveness is often anticipated by rebellious disobedience during latency age. As we shall see in the next chapter, non-authoritarian children tend to conform to normative expectations at this stage and later develop a capacity for more autonomous judgement. The authoritarian transition from destructiveness to conformity represents a further regression rather than moral development. It is a transition from raw, unmitigated, "uncontained" aggression and protest to righteous, moralistic and legalist-formalistic cruelty. While aggression can be construed as an authentic protest, conformity is the true self's admission of defeat. According to Winnicott (1966), the child's "antisocial acts" are meant to compel "society to go back with him or her to the position where things went wrong, and to acknowledge the fact".

The authoritarian personality abides by conventions to gain recognition, win the approval of hegemony and use these conventions as means for the exclusion of others. The invocation of principles is hypocritical and phony.[47] Authoritarian conformity assumes different

---

[46] *See also* Horkheimer (1949, 373).

[47] Not unlike other authoritarian statements of emotion and belief. Adorno often stressed this phoniness: "The sentimentality of the common people is by no means primitive, unreflecting emotion. On the contrary, it is pretense, a fictitious,

forms in different social orders. Mosse refers to the authoritarian conformity of the modern bourgeois order as *respectability*. He argues forcefully that German fascism, caught in the conflict between its claim to respectability and its inherent sexual licentiousness, opted for respectability and channeled sexuality into the erotization of the nation and its values. "Nationalism helped control sexuality, yet also provided the means through which changing sexual attitudes could be absorbed and tamed into respectability". (Mosse 1985, 10)

The authoritarian resort to conventions of respectability obeys, then, the exigencies of ego weakness. It is non-autonomous and destructive. Irrational and arbitrary parental attitudes prevent the full internalization of values as reasons for action.[48] "Due to the lack of genuine identification with the parents, the fearfully conforming child does not make the important developmental step from mere social anxiety to real conscience..." (Frenkel-Brunswick 1954, 237) On the socio-historical level, Hegel noted, cruelty forms an essential part of a social order that is based on rigid, abstract and formal obedience to principles, as opposed to real *ethical life* (Hegel 1977c, 293). Fromm and Winnicott suggest that authoritarian conformity compensates for the lack of a secure identity. The sought-after identity is dramatically discovered, at last, in some amalgam of social conventions. The authoritarian personality clings to random pieces of convention and tradition as substitutes for authentic spaces of familiarity and integrity, spaces of recognition and being-at-home-in-the-world. At some point and to a mild extent, every individual artificially reconstructs spaces of living once they lost some of their original grip and excitement. However, for the authoritarian personality, all social rules and values are, almost like the rules of rituals, external and artificial, devoid of the internal Reason that motivates non-authoritarian people to preserve their traditional forms of everyday life. Real conservatism is non-authoritarian. It is placed firmly within social structure and celebrates good and strong attachments and their cultural reifications.[49]

---

shabby imitation of real feeling, often self conscious and slightly contemptuous of itself." (Adorno 1946, 132) *See also* Adorno (1978, 137). See *The Authoritarian Personality* (Adorno *et al.* 1950, 418) on the lack of intrinsic worth of friendship.

[48] According to Erikson (1950, 80, 220), only if trust is established in the first developmental stage, can autonomy develop satisfactorily in the second.

[49] "Surprisingly or not, socialism thus turns out to be intrinsically conservative."

Authoritarian destructiveness and opportunism led Adorno and his collaborators to refer to authoritarian conformity as pseudoconservatism. They found a relatively low correlation between fascism (F-scale) and conservatism (PEC-scale). Authoritarian personalities are referred to as pseudoconservative since they show "blatant contradictions between their acceptance of all kinds of conventional and traditional values – by no means only in the political sphere – and their simultaneous acceptance of the more destructive clusters of the F-scale, such as, cynicism, punitiveness, and violent anti-Semitism" (Adorno *et al.* 1950, 683). Authoritarian personalities are not true conservatives because "...though [the fascist-minded person] seeks, or pretends to seek, the preservation of culture, the methods he advocates reveal that in fact he does not care whether it is preserved or destroyed and is unconsciously beset by highly destructive wishes" (Horkheimer 1950, 230). Fascist agitators, for example, "...violate the taboos which middle-class society has put upon any expressive behavior on the part of the normal, matter-of-fact citizen" (Adorno 1946, 131).

While internalized values reflect successful mature identifications that enrich and strengthen the ego, pseudoconservatism reflects failed, still longed-for, identification.

> ...the 'pseudo' traits are characteristic of those whose authoritarian identification succeeded only on a superficial level. They are forced to overdo it continuously in order to convince themselves and the others that they belong... to the right strata of society... The identification that failed is probably in most cases that with the father. Those people in whom this failure does not result in any real antagonism to authority, who accept the authoritarian pattern without, however, internalizing it, are likely to be those who identify themselves sociologically with higher social groups.... The goal toward which the pseudoconservative mentality strives – diffusely and semiconsciously – is to establish a dictatorship of the economically strongest group. (Adorno *et al.* 1950, 683-85)[50]

The authoritarian relation to norms is not one of consistent and

---

(Mueller 1982, 161)

[50] As Frenkel-Brunswick writes later, "The type of conformity displayed by parents of ethnocentric adolescents does not always consist in a genuine identification with traditional values. Our previous evidence already pointed to the fact that the authoritarian person has frequently lost his traditional roots and has made an attempt to compensate for this loss by non-functional forced and rigid conformity." (1954, 235, 265)

rational adherence but narcissistically opportunistic.[51] Fromm identifies this narcissistic feature in the Nazi party and its leadership when he observes that "Nazism never had any genuine political or economic principles. It is essential to understand that the very principle of Nazism is its radical opportunism" (Fromm 1941, 220). As Peter Wiles (1969, 167) notes, populism's "ideology is loose, and attempts to define it exactly arouse derision and hostility". The most ruthless communist leader differs from the fascist leader insofar as his legitimacy is grounded in principle and embodied in a social structure.[52] As Adorno observes,

> Totalitarianism means knowing no limits, not allowing for any breathing spell, conquest with absolute domination, complete extermination of the chosen foe. With regard to this meaning of fascist 'dynamism', any clear-cut program would function as a limitation, a kind of guarantee even to the adversary. It is essential to totalitarian rule that nothing shall be guaranteed, no limit is set to ruthless arbitrariness. (Adorno 1946, 128)

Adorno reveals the destructiveness that underlies authoritarian opportunism:

> ...destructiveness as the psychological basis of the fascist spirit. The programs are abstract and vague, the fulfillments are spurious and illusory because the promise expressed by fascist oratory is nothing but destruction itself... (Adorno 1946, 137)

In Israel, Begin's concern – from the mid-Fifties till the end of his career – for civility, democracy, welfare and liberty was entirely ostentatious and opportunistic.

> Begin's natural environment was the public political gathering. Here he gave himself full rein. At such times Begin did not so much deliver an orderly address as let himself be swept away in an extravaganza of words and gesticulations. Here solemnity vanished, as did the rules of international law and Latin phraseology. Although the left had a place in national unity, in the city square it became a bag to be punched and

---

[51] On the authoritarian personality's uncritical endorsement of social conventions see *The Authoritarian Personality* (Adorno *et al.* 1950, 429-30), Horkheimer (1949, 368, 373) and Frenkel-Brunawick (1954, 240-41).

[52] See Kershaw (1997) on the differences between Hitlerist and Stalinist régimes. These are nothing but the differences between non-structural and structural types of leadership.

punched again. (Shapiro 1991, 219)

Cynical and shrewd, Begin and his entourage posed as concerned with the welfare of Sepharadic Jews. However, "[i]n domestic policy, Begin was thoroughly eclectic – both populist and liberal... Expedient considerations and a desperate search for political alliance compelled Herut [Begin's party] not to abandon its commitment to the middle class, free enterprise, and some liberal principles" (Shapiro 1991, 80-83). Shapiro shows how Jabotinsky, the founding father and the eternal icon of the Israeli right, demanded the repudiation of any socio-economic interest in the face of national interest.[53] Shapiro notes that insincere manipulation of socio-economic unrest is characteristic of right wing parties everywhere. Equally insincere is the right wing's alleged concern for individual liberty. The destructive hate of the socialist establishment was mythologized as a struggle for liberty, and Jabotinsky as the noble knight of individual freedom. Shapiro observes that Jabotinsky conceived of individual freedom as actualized via the pursuit of national goals.[54] Democracy only became one of Begin's sacred values when it offered him convenient modes of political action, while in the first few years of Israel's statehood, Begin – whose personal authority within his party rested on terror, defamation of opponents and endless manipulations – and his assistants considered a violent *coup-d'état*.

Principles are invoked by fascist leaders engaged in legalistic argumentation only to aid them play the roles of peace-seeking victims and messengers of justice.[55] In Silone's dialogue, *School for Dictators,* one is taught how to treat political plans and programs. Thomas the Cynic, the sole perceptive participant in the dialogue, declaims:

> I admit that in a healthy political life competition between the parties would take the form of their presenting opposing political and economic

---

[53] "Harmonious relations must prevail between workers and employers, Jabotinsky writes, who will be guided by the principle that the national interest supersedes every class or sectoral interest." (Shapiro 1991, 19)

[54] "Jabotinsky accepted this argument in the years when he was influenced by the radical-right doctrine that spread rapidly through Europe in the inter-war period. His argument was consistent with the notion of these circles that true freedom is inner freedom and that the superiority of the nation is merely an expression of inner awareness of self realization." (Shapiro 1991, 12)

[55] See Erich Fromm (1975, 449) on the way Hitler rationalized his destructive urges in terms of moral duties.

> programs. But fascism is born in an entirely different atmosphere. Of course, it makes immediate claims, with all kinds of slogans, to win the support of the social forces that it needs; but apart from that it is careful not to formulate a constructive program. In its stead, fascism proposes an ideology formed of symbols of race and nation. If you are aiming at success, Mr. Double You, you must follow this rule: throw discredit on the traditional party system and on politics itself, make them responsible for all the nation's ills and rouse the hatred of the masses against them. (Silone 1964, 88)

Good and Bad Internal Objects

The authoritarian position, its roots in maternal misrecognition and its various characteristics, can be explained in Kleinian terms which complement and enrich the essentially Freudian account of the Frankfurt School. Some of the mechanisms and manifestations of authoritarianism – such as, the various aspects of maternal misrecognition, weak ego-boundaries, authoritarian sado-masochism, idealization, massive projection of aggression, paranoia, the sheer destructiveness to which Fromm referred as "necrophilia" (1975), self-hate and the vengeful hatred of liberalism and socialism – can be described in Kleinian terms more neatly than in Freudian terms. The language of Kleinian theory is more precise in some cases, and in others just lends itself to intuitive and convenient application in political psychology. Kleinian concepts were already integrated into the introductory definition and exposition of the three positions and the account of the authoritarian position at the beginning of the present chapter employed mainly Kleinian notions. Klein herself touched on problems of political psychology even less than Freud had done. The following account is no more than a construal of a Kleinian approach to authoritarianism based on the work of some of her disciples.

In Kleinian theory, the initial condition for individuation is ego identification with a firmly introjected good maternal object. The object-world of the authoritarian personality is marked by a lack of a strong introjected good maternal object that secures development out of fusion towards individuation. The result is an excessive dependence on paranoid-schizoid defense mechanisms. Klein's account of schizoid-paranoid mechanisms as permanent strategies of the ego, which are always in some use and excessively so during periods of regression, counts among her most important contributions.[56] The concepts of schizoid-paranoid mechanisms, good self, bad self and object-world, and the relation between recognition and integration, are indispensable for our comprehension of authoritarianism.

The introjection of dominant good objects depends on an adequate maternal recognition.

> All the enjoyments which the baby lives through in relation to his mother are so many proofs to him that the loved object *inside as well as outside* is not injured, is not turned into a vengeful person. The increase of love and trust, and the diminishing of fears through happy experiences, help the baby step by step to overcome his depression and feeling of loss (mourning). They enable him to test his inner reality by means of outer reality. Through being loved and through the enjoyment and comfort he has in relation to people his confidence in his own as well as other people's goodness becomes strengthened, his hope that his 'good' objects and his own ego can be saved and preserved increases, at the same time as his ambivalence and acute fears of internal destruction diminish. (Klein 1940, 149-50)

This process is extended to the incorporation of paternal objects. A fully developed, 'good' object-world will comprise maternal as well as paternal objects. The establishment of good internal objects is a long process interrupted by repeated regressions; it requires continuous recognition. It may take a while until maternal and paternal recognition or misrecognition, which structure the three positions, are decisively established. According to Klein, good objects can easily turn into persecutory objects that threaten the infant with annihilation, and persecutory objects can turn into good objects, until their dominant significance is determined.

> The desire to control the object, the sadistic gratification of overcoming and humiliating it, of getting the better of it, the *triumph* over it, may enter so strongly into the act of reparation (carried out by thoughts, activities, and sublimations) that the benign circle started by this act becomes broken. The objects which were to be restored change again into persecutors, and in turn paranoid fears are revived. These fears reinforce the paranoid defence mechanisms (of destroying the object) as well as the manic mechanisms (of controlling it or keeping it in suspended animation, and so on). The reparation which was in progress

---

[56] "Splitting, omnipotence, idealization, denial and control of internal and external objects are dominant at that stage." (Klein, 1952, 70)

> is thus disturbed or even nullified – according to the extent to which these mechanisms are activated. As a result of the failure of the act of reparation, the ego has to resort again and again to obsessional and manic defences. (Klein 1940, 153)

Klein accepts Freud's structural theory with some reservations. She lays emphasis on the object-world that exists alongside the ego and influences its nature. She antedates the origins of the ego and super-ego in relation to Freud's periodization. According to Kleinian theory, the authoritarian super-ego would look much the way it was conceived by the authors of *The Authoritarian Personality*: unintegrated, persecutory and repressive. However, the origin of the authoritarian super-ego would be traced much further back, to the earliest persecutory objects consolidated by an ongoing maternal misrecognition.[57]

The schizoid-paranoid split is a defensive personality organization, inevitable at the beginning of life. No external stimulus is needed to prompt it but to alleviate it. According to Klein, failure to institute a firm, good internal object precipitates an oft-repeated recourse to schizoid-paranoid splitting of the ego and the object-world in order to protect the good object by keeping it apart from the persecutory object. Klein's concepts readily explain the defensive, fearful posture of authoritarianism. Primary fusion is schizoid-*paranoid.*[58] In Bion's terms, authoritarian paranoia can be seen as a result of a failure of maternal "containment." Maternal misrecognition produces paranoia not only because hatred is over-stimulated, but, once projected onto a persecutory external object, it is only aggravated instead of being contained and mitigated by him.

Donald Meltzer has argued that factors listed by Klein – persecution and intolerance of depressive anxieties[59] – are insufficient to produce the

---

[57] Klein writes: "... in the first few months of its life the child goes through paranoid anxieties related to the 'bad' denying breasts, which are felt as external and internalized persecutors..." (1935, 140)

[58] Authoritarian paranoia was already described in *The Authoritarian Personality.* Frenkel-Brunswick and Sanford (1946, 114) report the paranoid imagination (stories of haunted houses, conspiracy theories) of interviewees high on the anti-Semitic-personality scale. For a recent Kleinian account of political paranoia see Robins and Post (1998). *See also* Storr (1991) and Berke *et al.* (1998).

[59] According to Klein, depressive anxieties appear with the attainment of separation-individuation and the realization of one's aggression towards the good

submissiveness to the persecutory object that defines authoritarianism. Meltzer argues that submission to a tyrannical bad object depends on the illusion that the latter protects the ego and on the accompanying "dread of loss of the illusory protection".

> It is important to note that, while the tyrant may behave in a way that has a resemblance to a persecutor, especially if any sign of rebellion is at hand, the essential hold over the submissive part of the self is by way of the dread of loss of protection against the terror. I have come to the conclusion that intolerance of depressive anxieties alone will not produce the addictive constellation of submission to the tyrant – nor in combination with persecution by the damaged object. (Meltzer 1968, 400)

The protective role of the persecutory object may not be entirely illusory. An object that is not extremely persecutory and one with which the ego can identify still enables the ego to maintain a certain personality organization. Meltzer is right to observe that illusion forms an important part in the submission to a tyrannical object. Paranoid fears are often coped with by denying or idealizing the internal persecutor.

> When persecution is too intense to be borne, it may be completely denied. Such magic denial is based on a phantasy of the total annihilation of the persecutors. Another way in which omnipotent denial may be used against excessive persecution is by idealizing the persecuting object itself, and treating it as ideal. Sometimes the ego identifies with this pseudo-ideal object. This kind of idealization and omnipotent denial of persecution is often seen in the analysis of schizoid patients, who present a history of having been 'perfect babies', never protesting and never crying, as though all experiences were experienced by them as good ones. In adult life, these mechanisms lead to lack of discrimination between good and bad, and to fixations upon bad objects that have to be idealized. (Segal 1973, 27)

External persecutory objects that correspond to internal objects, such as authoritarian parents, are also idealized. Fairbairn considered the idealization of external objects as a constitutive event: internal objects result from the introjection of external objects' aggression in the course of idealization. External aggression is denied, the external object is exonerated and idealized. At times, denials of persecution may have some positive results. To a certain extent they may temper persecution and help accept, control and manipulate inner and external reality. Denial

---

maternal object which made separation-individuation possible in the first place.

and idealization are mainly described by Klein as features of the manic defense. One of her remarks on denial in that context aptly describes the authoritarian denial in question:

> ...my observations have led me to conclude that this mechanism of denial originates in that very early phase in which the undeveloped ego endeavors to defend itself from the most overpowering and profound anxiety of all, namely, its dread of internalized persecutors and of the id. (Klein 1935, 132)

However, authoritarian idealization and denial do not necessarily coincide with the manic defense, at least according to the Kleinian account of the latter. The manic defense, unlike authoritarian idealization, is said usually to assume proximity to a firm good object with whom the ego can identify. It is employed by strong rather than weak egos, playing a positive role in the strengthening of the ego in the course of its working-through the depressive position. Furthermore, in the manic defense, it is the ego rather than the bad object that is idealized and equated with the ego ideal (Klein 1940). The authoritarian idealization of the bad object may culminate in a manic moment of ego identification with the idealized object. However, it would be difficult to sustain such a manic identification since its foundations are precarious.

In "Notes on Some Schizoid Mechanisms" and *Envy and Gratitude,* Klein discusses yet another type of idealization: not of the ego nor of the bad object but of the good object. Klein's ideas on this kind of idealization enhance, by way of analogy, our understanding of authoritarian idealization. First, authoritarian idealization may also contain an implicit evocation of a lost longing for a love-relation to a good, total object. "While idealization is thus the corollary of persecutory fear, it also springs from the power of the instinctual desires which aim at unlimited gratification...". (Klein 1946, 182) Second, Klein's explanation of hallucinatory gratification as a kind of idealization seems to apply to familiar authoritarian forms of phony gratification.

> In hallucinatory gratification, therefore, two interrelated processes take place: the omnipotent conjuring up of the ideal object and situation, and the equally omnipotent annihilation of the bad persecutory object and the painful situation. These processes are based on splitting both the object and the ego. (Klein 1957, 192)

Idealization of authoritarian parents was noted by both Kleinian theorists and by the authors of *The Authoritarian Personality.* The Kleinian tradition offers its own perspective on personalities founded on a lie, such as, the idealization of childhood, of hated parents and of badness. The Kleinian perspective suggests a general, not context-specific, understanding of *ideology* as idealization of bad objects.[60] In authoritarian idealization, self-hate stemming from the predominance of the bad self is also repressed. In order to appease the persecutory object, avoid integration and perpetuate split, these personalities inflict pain upon themselves. They may avoid emotional relationships (which imply integration), frustrate the efforts of people trying to help them, resist rehabilitation and return to crime, prison and poverty. They are likely to vote for an authoritarian leader against their own interests. The authoritarian personality seeks authority which corresponds to the internal persecutory object and which, particularly in the political sphere, must be idealized.

Idealization of the bad object does not spare the authoritarian personality from self-hate. Klein's and Fairbairn's notions of the bad self and the bad object, which were not available to the Frankfurt School, capture the pattern of self-hate produced by authoritarian parenting. One of the first articles which analyzed masochism from a Kleinian perspective was Berliner's "The Role of Object Relations in Moral Masochism" (1958). Berliner captures the essence of authoritarian masochism as a search for an idealized sadistic object accompanied by a denial of hatred towards this object. Berliner traces masochism to early object relations:

> The defense mechanisms involved are primarily denial and libidinization of suffering. The experience of hate and ill-treatment is repressed. The child, in its imperative need for love, accepts this hate and ill treatment as if they were love and is not conscious of the difference. Suffering thus libidinized is introjected. (Berliner 1958, 44)

The desperate authoritarian hatred of individualism, socialism and elitism combines a vindictive envy of strong good objects with fear of the destabilizing consequences that a social principle of universal recognition would have on the authoritarian personality organization. "In the eyes of the European radical right, socialism was the most implacable foe of the national movement." (Shapiro 1991, 52) Theweleit models this envious hate on the envy felt towards privileged and dispossessing young

---

[60] In a broader sense, ideology may refer to any idealization of traditions to which one is attached.

brothers.[61] Fascism, for its own part, never takes its social programs and slogans seriously.[62]

The authoritarian personality avoids integration and rehabilitation for several reasons. According to Klein, split is intended to protect weak good objects when the good self is sensed to be too impoverished to sustain integration. The good object's hushed voice can sometimes be briefly heard when the assertiveness of the idealized, dominant bad object temporarily crumbles. Rosenfeld writes that "the narcissistic organization not only increases the strength of the destructive narcissism, but it has a defensive purpose to keep itself in power and so maintain the status quo" (Rosenfeld 1971, 174).

Split is not only meant to secure the bad object's rule but it is an exercise of the bad object's own defensive sadism. The bad self is revengeful and envious of the good self's self-love and integrative powers. The bad self originates in frustration and typically contains a contradiction between this formative dissatisfaction and its idealized and inflated super-ego. This contradiction seems to make the bad self all the more fragile and defensive *vis-à-vis* the relatively harmonious good self. Alice Miller, in her analysis of Hitler, illustrates how persecution of the weak good self extends to external weak objects:

> The persecution of the Jews permitted him to *persecute* the weak child in his own self that was now projected onto the victims. In this way he would not have to experience grief over his past pain, which had been especially hard to bear because his mother had not been able to prevent it. (Miller 1983, 190)

Furthermore, split is perpetuated because the unintegrated bad object becomes loved, an object of perverse, addictive, masochistic narcissism. Finally, split enables the bad object to retain its delusions of omnipotence.

---

[61] The authoritarian hatred of socialists and communists is a recurring theme in Theweleit's *Male Phantasies*. *See*, for example, Theweleit (1989, 378-80). On the role of brotherhood in authoritarian fantasy see Adorno (1978, 131) and Brooker (1991). The subject still awaits a separate psychoanalytic study.

[62] See the discussion above of the authoritarian crowd's masochism. National-socialist fear of socialism is demonstrated by the systematic purging of the party of its socialist elements, such as Strasser. *See also* Silone (1964, 134-35). On the indifference of Italian fascism to socio-economic issues see Fromm (1991, 248).

> The narcissistic organization is in my experience not primarily directed against guilt and anxiety, but seems to have the purpose of maintaining the idealization and superior power of the destructive narcissism. To change, to receive help, implies weakness and is experienced as wrong or as failure by the destructive narcissistic organization which provides the patient with his sense of superiority. In cases of this kind there is a most determined chronic resistance to analysis and only the very detailed exposure to the system enables analysis to make some progress. (Rosenfeld 1971, 174) [63]

When the path of separation-individuation is not taken, as in the case of the authoritarian personality, omnipotent symbiotic longings dominate. The longing to disappear into and fuse with land, nation and national symbols is characteristic of the authoritarian personality. The orientation of the authoritarian personality outwards, its fragile boundaries, search for authority and tendency to identify with and immerse itself in a variety of external objects, is anticipated in the Kleinian conception of split and weak ego. Rosenfeld, following Klein, speaks of "...projective and introjective identification of self and object (fusion of self and object) in narcissistic states, which act as a defence against any recognition of separateness between the self and objects" (Rosenfeld 1971, 172). This is the malignant narcissism that characterizes the authoritarian personality, as opposed to the mature, 'secondary' narcissism that characterizes the reconciled position.[64] According to Klein, the weak-ego is prone to indiscriminate identifications and excessive use of projective identification.

> [The strong ego] becomes less liable to identify indiscriminately with a variety of objects, a process that is characteristic of a weak ego.... When things go wrong, excessive projective identification, by which split-off parts of the self are projected into the object, leads to a strong confusion between the self and the object, which also comes to stand for the self. Bound up with this is a weakening of the ego and a grave disturbance in object relations. (Klein 1957, 192)[65]

---

[63]The same analysis can be found in Rosenfeld (1990, 87,88,106,109).

[64] There are also differences between reconciled and alienated forms of narcissism. Every position corresponds to a different type of narcissism.

[65] In a brief remark in the end of her "Contribution to the Psychogenesis of Manic-Depressive States" (1935) Klein mentions flights to external objects as an attempt to overcome the agonies of the depressive position. In other writings she

The Kleinian perspective reveals the role of the mother in the formation of authoritarianism and suggests convincing explanations of many authoritarian phenomena. Furthermore, Klein's perspective highlights authoritarian effects of maternal misrecognition which were not considered by the authors of *The Authoritarian Personality*. These authoritarian characteristics constitute an additional authoritarian syndrome, which will be described in the next section.

Narcissistic Authoritarianism

The image of the authoritarian character produced by Horkheimer, Adorno and their associates suffers from a certain lack of cohesiveness. It seems to confound two different authoritarian prototypes. If the position of the authoritarian personality is defined by want of maternal recognition, this want can assume different forms which correspond to different manifestations of authoritarianism. Horkheimer and the authors of *The Authoritarian Personality*, in their fleeting remarks on the mother's authoritarian attitude, described it as conforming to the pattern of paternal authoritarianism. The child is inescapably confronted with uniform parental authoritarianism. In such cases, maternal misrecognition is a pale shadow of the paternal attitude. The resounding paternal authoritarian voice is echoed by the mother. The mother does not allow the child to stand up against the father, overtly or covertly, and simultaneously reinforces the impression of the paternal attitude.

Kleinian and post-Kleinian thinking reveals that it is not only when the maternal attitude is one of uniformity with an authoritarian father that it amounts to misrecognition and results in ego weakness and sado-masochistic authoritarianism. When the mother assertively claims the infant's self she does not allow the infant to complete individuation-separation processes. In one set of scenarios, maternal misrecognition typically consists of scarcity of warmth and responsiveness. In the second, while there is no apparent lack of warmth and responsiveness on the mother's part, the mother is too possessive, narcissistic, violent, seductive and disempowering. The notions of a phallic mother, castrating mother or Klein's "mother with a penis," namely, a mother at once masculine and feminine, readily come to mind.

---

further refers to flight mechanisms.

Let us refer to authoritarianism produced by the second type of maternal misrecognition as *narcissistic authoritarianism* (though, in a wider sense, all forms of authoritarianism share a regressive narcissistic aspiration to eliminate structure). Fromm has identified a similar, specific form of authoritarianism, related to an ongoing symbiotic attachment to the mother.[66]

The life-long role of the maternal imago has been observed by numerous students of mythology and psychoanalysts. No matter what the eventual balance between its loving and persecutory aspects is, the imago of an omnipotent mother remains all-important (Klein 1957, 185). Klein's entire theory is based on the splitting of the maternal imago into persecutory and benevolent objects, as one of its fundamental assumptions. Students of mythology have deciphered representations of the malevolent and benevolent aspects of the Mother imago in the figures of mythical goddesses and in a wealth of symbols.[67] To take an obvious example, the sexual, bisexual, incestuous and lethal aspects of the Mother imago, as well as the aspect of the mother's body as an infinite body of which we are made and which retains its identity through us as its extensions, find expression in the frequent evocations of earth as a maternal symbol.

In cases of maternal misrecognition, it is the persecutory and morbid

---

[66] Fromm (1975, 402-4) refers to the "necrophile" character. Grunberger and Dessuant (1997) discuss the narcissist basis of some manifestations of anti-Semitism.

[67] See Bachhofen's (1973) interpretations of Demeter and Aphrodite as two maternal principles; Jung (1982, 109-10) on the ambivalence of the maternal imago; Friedrich (1978) on the fusion of the maternal and the sexual; Lévêque (1997, ch. 1, 2) on the life-giving and the deadly aspects of the maternal goddesses. In his book, *The Great Mother* (1955), Erich Neumann has articulated the benevolent as well as dangerous and possessive persecutory aspects of the mother imago on the basis of a thorough survey of maternal symbols across many cultures. *See also* Neumann (1994). Fromm (1975, 403-4) writes on the personality to which we refer as 'narcissistic authoritarian': "For them mother is a symbol: a phantom rather than a real person. She is a symbol of earth, of home, of blood, of race, of nation, of the deepest ground from which life emerges and to which it returns. But she is also the symbol of chaos and death; she is not the life-giving mother, but the death-giving mother; her embrace is death, her womb is a tomb... I have found clinically that the fear of the destructive mother is by far more intense than of the punishing, castrating father." *See also* James (1959).

aspects of the Mother imago that are heightened. Slater has studied the maternal imago which specifically corresponds to the possessive and narcissistic type of maternal misrecognition. He reconstructed the nature of narcissistic mothering in ancient Greece drawing on knowledge of Greek material culture and mythology. According to Slater, Greek mothers avenged their social subjugation on their sons, using them as their own extensions in order to realize their aspirations. Slater invokes Bateson's concept of double-bind to describe the Greek mother's demands on her son: "(1) You must be a strong and adult male, treat me as a woman, and by your conspicuous male achievements express my own aspirations. (2) You must not aspire to maleness nor flaunt your masculinity before me nor remind me that I am a woman. (3) You must not desert me nor find any contradiction in my demands." (Slater 1992, 50) Whether or not double-bind is the major psychological outcome of these demands, Slater seems right to relate them to maternal narcissism. His findings strongly support the correlation between the mother's and the son's narcissism: narcissism is often related to deficient nurturing, to "close physical mother-son contact" during periods of sexual deprivation and to distant marital relationship between the parents (Slater 1992, 436-38). Though Slater does not elaborate on the political implications of narcissism, he remarks that narcissism is closely related to authoritarianism (Slater 1992, 444) and his description of the former illuminates the nature of narcissistic authoritarianism.

Slater speculates on the ways in which narcissistic mothering and aggressive maternal imago produce narcissistic character traits:

> What binds together homosexuality, schizophrenia, and the need for achievement is a deep concern and doubt about the integrity and value – not in moral terms but in something closer to a monetary sense – of the self. We call this concern, together with the various devices developed to obviate it, narcissism. I have tried to show that its roots lie in an overloaded mother-child relationship that prevents the development of clear but flexible and permeable boundaries. (Slater 1992, 454)

Primary, narcissistic symbiosis is prolonged. Individuation-separation processes do not progress; mother and self are alternately felt to be entirely inside or outside.[68] The total immersion and imprisonment in the

---

[68] Kohut (1971, 37-57) traces narcissism to a failure of mature introjection and a resulting fixation on an early symbiotic relation. For the same view of narcissism see Mahler (1979).

symbiotic bond are expressed by the totalization and aesthetization of experience and in the longing for total bliss. This longing, together with the need to flee from ruthlessly destructive internal objects and the enigmatic nature of the repressed truth, account for the mystical moments of fascism, as attempts at absolute, irrational transportation.[69] Symbiosis is temporarily materialized in the state of *communitas* that follows an authoritarian overthrow of structure. In *communitas*, the symbiotic bond is re-lived and the persecutory imago is enacted in self-mutilation, mock combats, sacrifice, suspension of sexual taboos and so on.

While the maternal attitude is loving-seducing, it does not encourage individuation because it demands admiration, obedience and exclusivity. The infant is recognized only *qua* an ally and extension of the mother.[70] The mother claims possession of the child's self and enjoyment. In Kleinian terms, it is a mother who "scoops" good objects and keeps them for herself, thus perpetuating the child's symbiotic dependence.

> ...the projection of good feelings and good parts of the self into the mother is essential for the infant's ability to develop good object-relations and to integrate his ego. However, if this projective process is carried out excessively, good parts of the personality are felt to be lost, and in this way the mother becomes the ego-ideal; this process too results in weakening and impoverishing the ego. Very soon such processes extend to other people, and the result may be an overstrong dependence on these external representatives of one's own good parts. (Klein 1946, 184)

The mother imago is all-inclusive. The child cannot separate love and hate in its relation to its mother.[71] The mother embodies both the

---

[69] Mystical doctrines refer explicitly to their root in a desperate apprehension of the intractable power of evil. On the conception of evil as an independent intractable power in the Gnosis and the Kabbalah, see Scholem (1974), to mention just one example. On narcissistic authoritarianism and mysticism see Adorno (1994) and Grunberger and Dessuant (1997). According to Reich, "...fascist mysticism is orgastic yearning, restricted by mystic distortion and inhibition of natural sexuality..." (1970, xxi).

[70] "The 'pervert's mother' plays temptress when she leads the child to believe that he has no need either to grow up or to identify with his father in order to be her perfect partner. This allows the child's ego ideal to become fixated at a level at which archaic ideals of fusion and oedipal victory predominate." (Chasseguet-Smirgel 1985, 33)

[71] On the envious infant's inability to separate love and hate, see Klein (1957,

maternal and paternal principles; she has been described as 'phallic' and castrating.[72] The mother, Klein suggests, is phallic because she is omnipotent, omnipresent and, as such, an object of envy.[73] If separation-individuation from the omnipotent mother is normally facilitated by the mother's phallic deficiency, it is clear why a mother who hampers separation would be conceived of as phallic.[74]

It has been argued that, in such cases, the child's relation to the mother is overtly sexual.[75] The infant is seduced to cling to the symbiotic bond and remains powerless to overcome it. Furthermore, only within the symbiotic bond can the narcissistic authoritarian's illusion that the bad object is good be preserved, and even then its constant idealization, appeasement and seduction are required. This continuing symbiotic dependence on a threatening maternal imago produces a longing for love, on the one hand, and a longing for safe isolation in the form of narcissistic pride, on the other.

The attraction to the death-mother could not be affection or love; it is not

---

184).

[72] On the phallic mother see Freud (1908, 1909, 1923a, 1923b). On the witch as a universal symbol of the phallic mother see Roheim (1950, 215). See also Klein (1945, 375, 411; 1952, 78-79) on the mother with a penis and on the maternal penis' hostility in retaliation to the infant's attacks. On the castrating mother see Karl Abraham (1920, 368-69) and Klein (1928, 190).

[73] According to Klein, greed and envy produce these imagoes of the phallic mother, the father with breast and so on (1952, 79).

[74] "Realization that possession of the penis presents the possibility of healing the narcissistic wound imposed by the omnipotent mother helps to explain some of the unconscious significance of the penis, whether it is that of a treasure of strength, integrity, magic power, or autonomy. In the idea connected with this organ we find condensed all the primitive ideas of power. This power becomes then the prerogative of the man, who by attracting the mother destroyed her power." (Chasseguet-Smirgel 1981, 116)

[75] "If the narcissistic confirmation is excessive, it may result in perverting development by preventing the ego ideal from being cathected in the genital father, as we have seen in the case of the pervert. In fact in this instance narcissistic confirmation is coupled with sexual seduction. The child is then, par excellence, the erotic 'plaything' Freud referred to, the sexual seduction itself constituting the narcissistic confirmation the child is so avid for: that he is a suitable partner for his mother and hence corresponds to his own ego ideal." (Chasseguet-Smirgel 1985, 31)

an attraction in the common psychological sense denoting something pleasant and warm,... she is the ocean in which he wants to drown, the ground in which he wants to be buried. (Fromm 1975, 403)

The narcissistic authoritarian differs in many respects from the authoritarian character described by the Frankfurt School. The narcissistic authoritarian character has stronger self to draw upon and inner objects which drive it to act and achieve. He may be ambitious, self-indulgent and may have artistic and intellectual aspirations, like those of Wagner, Hitler and Mussolini. Indeed, it is often the narcissistic authoritarian who would strive to lead the authoritarian mass. According to Winnicott, "*[o]ne of the roots of the need to be dictator may be a compulsion to deal with this fear of woman by encompassing her and acting for her.* The dictator's curious habit of demanding not only absolute obedience and absolute dependence but also 'love' can be derived from this source" (1965, 165).[76] The illusory omnipotence lavished by the initial symbiotic bond cannot be relinquished.

Slater characterizes the narcissistic character as extremely sensitive to public insult, boastful, bloodthirsty and engaged in the pursuit of glory and acclaim (Slater 1992, 420). He quotes Finely's suggestion that "[n]othing defines the quality of Greek culture more neatly than the way in which the idea of competition was extended from physical prowess to the realm of the intellect, to feats of poetry and dramatic composition" (Slater 1992, 36).[77] Various theorists of narcissism have described the narcissist's fluctuations between grandiose self-esteem and self-hate.

...just as the object-instinctual experiences of the Oedipal period become the prototype of our later object-instinctual involvements and form the basis for our specific weaknesses and strengths in this area, so do the experiences during the period of the formation of the self become the prototype of the specific forms of our later vulnerability and security in

---

[76] Winnicott continues: "Moreover, the tendency of groups of people to accept or even seek *actual* domination is derived from a fear of domination by *fantasy woman.* This fear leads them to seek, and even welcome, domination by a known human being, especially one who has taken on himself the burden of personifying and therefore limiting the magical qualities of the all-powerful woman of fantasy, to whom is owed a great debt. The dictator can be overthrown, and must eventually die; but the woman figure of primitive unconscious fantasy had no limits to her existence or power..."

[77] The quotation is from Finely (1959, 128-29).

> the narcissistic realm: of the ups and downs in our self esteem; of our lesser or greater need for praise, for merger into idealized figures, and for other forms of narcissistic sustenance; and of the greater or lesser cohesion of our self during periods of transition, whether in the transition to latency, in early or late adolescence, in maturity, or in old age. (Kohut 1973, 368-69)

Chasseguet-Smirgel described the compulsion to idealize oneself as stemming from the same symbiotic relation to the mother which seems to produce narcissistic authoritarianism.[78] Coldness is reversed into promiscuous sentimentality[79] and destructiveness into pseudo-erudite legalistic argumentation.[80] Fromm notes how Hitler's rhetoric assumes

---

[78] "Through the idealization of his instincts and his part objects, the pervert achieves a sort of narcissistic fulfillment since this leads to an idealization of his own ego... In this way he manages to approximate more nearly the time when he was his own ideal. He admires himself in his glorified instincts, in his exalted objects, as he used to admire himself in his mother's eyes, where he sought confirmation of his adorable perfection. However, the ever-present possibility that the disguise making the infantile and truncated nature of his ego will be seen through, makes him particularly exigent as to the quality of all that surrounds him, particularly in the aesthetic sphere. He will seek out the most exquisite curios, the most accomplished works of art, the most well-turned poems, the most refined decor." (1985, 23)

[79] According to Klein, narcissistic symbiotic object relations "...may lead to a compulsive tie to certain objects or – another outcome – to a shrinking from people in order to prevent both a destructive intrusion into them and the danger of retaliation by them" (Klein 1946, 187). According to Rosenfeld, "[i]n the narcissistic states where the libidinal aspects predominate destructiveness becomes apparent as soon as the omnipotent self-idealization is threatened by contact with an object which is perceived as separate from the self." (Rosenfeld 1971, 173) Likewise, according to Kernberg, "The coldness and aloofness of patients with pathological narcissism – when their capacity for social charm is not put into action – the tendency to disregard others except in temporary idealization of potential sources of narcissistic supply, and the prevalence of contempt and devaluation in most of their relationships are in marked contrast to the warm quality of the small child's self centeredness. Pursuing this observation into the historical analysis of narcissistic patients, one finds from the age of two to three years an impressive lack of normal warmth and engagement with others and an easily activated destructiveness and ruthlessness, which is abnormal." (Kernberg 1974, 259).

[80] On authoritarian feigned erudition, see Adorno (1994, 118).

that "[h]e and the German people are always the ones who are innocent and the enemies are sadistic brutes" (Fromm 1941, 228). Revengefulness and destructiveness are reversed into affected kindness: "Hitler was in a way a grotesque figure: a man driven by the passion to destroy, a man without compassion, a volcano of archaic passions – trying to appear a well-bred, considerate, even harmless gentleman" (Fromm 1975, 473).[81]

Shapiro illustrates fascist affectation in his illuminating analysis of Begin's leadership:

> Begin entered Israel's political scene as a nationalist revolutionary. Years would pass before he would change his image – the parliamentarian who observes all the rules, the gentleman who awaits his turn, was a much later arrival on the scene.... By the time Ben-Gurion resigned the premiership in June 1963, Begin had taken his first steps towards erasing the stigma of delegitimation with which he had been branded from the time he entered the political arena. Instead of the revolutionary hurling challenges at the political order, on to the scene came the gentleman and parliamentarian with clemency to his rivals, advocating the unity of the nation and representation of the general interests of the people. (Shapiro 1991, 79-83)

Power is envied bitterly and any insult provokes vengeful rage. While *The Road to Power* may be long, the narcissistic authoritarian person pursues vendettas with unshakable decisiveness (Kohut 1973). "Another factor in Hitler's impressiveness was his narcissism and the unshakable *certainty* that, like so many narcissists, he felt about his ideas." (Fromm

---

[81] See also the discussion of authoritarian charismatic leadership in the previous section of this chapter. Kohut describes the pseudoconservative hypocritic resolution of the tension between moral respectability and narcissistic self-assertion as follows: "Many of those in Germany who could no longer maintain their narcissistic equilibrium were ready to see in Hitler and in the National Socialist Party a chance for the deployment of the narcissism of the archaic grandiose self to which they had regressed. This was possible because Hitler's programs, though clearly promising the fulfillment of the crudest narcissistic aims of power and domination, were yet disguised, however thinly, as a system of ideals. In other words, the Nazi propagandists and the framers of the Nazi ideology (like the obscurantist Hans Rosenberg) claimed that they were motivated by the highest ideals. The very frenzy, however, with which the leader figure was extolled, the emphasis on his absolute power and his omniscience, betrayed that he was not a symbol for values but that he represented a concretization of the grandiose self of the masses." (Kohut 1985a, 67)

1975, 461)[82] The mother's own actual and desired virility, her genitalization of her child and the view of the father as a model for one's own desired emancipation from the mother (Slater 1992, 49), all produce an unlimited respect for masculinity – usually in its most conventional interpretations, – a hatred of one's own femininity[83] and of femininity in general.

As we saw in this last section, maternal misrecognition, generative of authoritarianism, can assume different forms. While most of the insights into the nature of authoritarianism were offered by Fromm, Horkheimer, Reich, Adorno and the authors of *The Authoritarian Personality*, a fuller conception of authoritarianism must draw on Kleinian insights which provide convincing explanations of various authoritarian phenomena and account in detail for the role of the mother in the formation of authoritarianism. The next chapter considers the theories of Freud and Klein, as well as those of Hegel and Mead, in the context of the reconciled position.

---

[82] As Silone (1964, 107) writes, "Whatever the fascist leader says must be said as if it were self-evident, so as not to leave room for the slightest doubt or argument."

[83] Slater (1992) offers interesting explanations of narcissistic femininity. He notes the oscillation in the appearance of Dionysos between a phallic bearded god and an effeminate figure (212). "The homosexual search posited by Abraham is in part a search for a more neutral, non-devouring protector, but it is also a search for a more heroic self-image. This is sought through a male identification and an attempted purging of maternally induced conflicts..." (55, see also 62-63). Slater also explains narcissistic homosexuality as a kind of identification with the mother-aggressor (377).

3. Reconciled Liberalism

The Reconciled Position

While there is no absolute correspondence in reality between any of the three positions and an ideological or party affiliation, the reconciled position is even more ideologically underdetermined than the other positions. Its structure compels its occupants to traverse a variety of political ideologies. The reconciled position gives rise to a spectrum of political ideologies or, more precisely, to a *developmental continuum* of reconciled political ideologies. The occupant of the reconciled position moves from one political ideology to another as he consolidates his individuation-separation.

The reconciled position is constituted by mutual recognition in both private and public spheres. The reconciled person enjoys sufficient responsiveness to establish individuation and mature identification in relation to the two spheres. Recognition fosters differentiation between the two spheres as complementary, mutually recognizing and mutually fertilizing spheres of existence. The reconciled liberal is reconciled to the intimacy of the private sphere and to the universality of the civic sphere, which, unlike the alienated liberal, he experiences as broadly continuous and coordinated spheres of interaction. Simultaneous identification with the two spheres involves tensions and narcissistic wounds known best to occupants of this position. Mature identification with both spheres constitutes an object-world which burdens and exhausts the ego, yet, one that promises social recognition and a potential for development. Occupants of the reconciled position identify with traditions and authorities that represent the two spheres.[1] It is a rich, complex and conflictual system of identifications which takes time and effort to stabilize. The brighter side of this laborious process is that the relation to the hegemonic order is non-paranoiac and trust-based, fostering an endorsement of communal values and the establishment of a secure ethical identity. Only the reconciled person can consistently identify with the Father, leader and society at large as an integrated and strongly individuated person.

The combination of private and civic recognition enables the reconciled liberal to establish mature narcissism that involves an empowering sense of membership, a seizure of territory in the social world and an ability to recognize and integrate one's own aggression.[2] The reconciled liberal attains a balance between the super-ego – the exacting, juridical and absent-transcendent aspect of internalized authority – and the narcissistic ego ideal. By contrast, the narcissism of the authoritarian personality is destructive, seeking to collapse structure. Social structure and deviant *communitas* – the reconciled and the authoritarian positions – correspond, then, to two alternative organizations of narcissism (Barshack 2000). The suspension of identity in rituals and in other forms of *communitas* responds to the primary narcissistic aspirations that are frustrated by structure. The individuation-separation process that underlies structure involves narcissistic wounds. It enjoins renunciation of early omnipotence and recognition of clear normative boundaries. Authoritarian *communitas* aims to revive the archaic symbiotic bond and to refuse the narcissistic costs inflicted in the course of separation-individuation. Such narcissism differs from the narcissistic realm of highly individuated personalities.

Firmly individuated, normative identities must have a positive narcissistic value, too, to make social structure possible.[3] Mature

---

[1] The maintenance of ego-strength depends on an ongoing availability of external counterparts to the inner object-world: external sources of recognition in the form of ethical traditions, institutions, reference-groups and concrete persons.

[2] In *Moses and Monotheism* Freud suggests that Jewish inability to acknowledge violence towards the Father results in the predominance of the exacting aspects of the super-ego.

[3] "We see a movement from archaic to mature narcissism, side by side and intertwined with a movement from archaic to mature object love; we do not see an abandonment of self-love and its replacement by the love of others." (Kohut

narcissism involves an easy sense of structural identity and love of authority. Kohut claims that only when mothering is deficient and fails to perform *selfobject* functions (which, according to Kohut, are 'mirroring', 'idealization' and 'twinship') does a fixation on the archaic, grandiose *selfobject* take place. Such a fixation produces a weak personality organization, one that is not properly individuated and that is hostile to structure, aspiring to spread and entrench ritual narcissism.[4]

The narcissistic *incorporation* that, according to Freud, is involved in identification suggests itself as a source of structural narcissism. According to Freud, the individuation-separation process involves the emergence of concrete identity through mature identifications. The normative identities, whose interrelationships make up social structures, originate in such identifications. In *Totem and Taboo*, Freud treats identification with the slaughtered primal father as the starting point of social structure, law and religion. Identifications inscribe lineage membership and, according to classical psychoanalysis, a 'normative order' in the crystallizing personality.

Authorities and traditions may set challenges and limits but at the same time they breed and nourish the narcissism of structure. Their Law is seductive and empowering. They breed narcissism by recognizing individuals as their extensions and by infusing individuals with their power, wisdom and grace. Authorities and traditions bestow the powers of descent: legitimacy and membership, and consequent economic, political and religious rights. Identification marks the beginning of the

---

1984, 208)

[4] Kohut describes the alternative potential processes: "Under favorable circumstances the neutralized forces emanating from the narcissistic self (the narcissistic needs of the personality and its ambitions) become gradually integrated into the web of our ego as a healthy enjoyment of our own activities and successes and as an adaptively useful sense of disappointment tinged with anger and shame over our failures and shortcomings. And, similarly, the ego ideal (the internalized image of perfection which we admire and to which we are looking up) may come to form a continuum with the ego, as a focus for our ego-syntonic values, as a healthy sense of direction and beacon for our activities and pursuits, and as an adaptively useful object of longing disappointment, when we cannot reach it. A firmly cathected, strongly idealized super ego absorbs considerable amounts of narcissistic energy, a fact which lessens the personality's propensity towards narcissistic imbalance. Shame, on the other hand, arises when the ego is unable to provide a proper discharge for the exhibitionistic demands of the narcissistic self." (1985a, 107)

appropriation of social territory in structure. Indeed, 'universal succession' is often referred to in legal language as 'identification' of the heir with the deceased. Through the concrete objects of their secondary identifications (father, mother), members of social structures identify with the big Other (Father, Mother) and jurally acquire social membership and territory.[5]

With individuation, the primary *Thing* splits into three sources of mature self-love: an *introjected* good object, a narcissistic *envelope*[6] and a *transcendent*, benevolent, recognizing big Other. Structural narcissism consists in the construction of the big Other through incorporation and simultaneous elevation of the primary Thing onto a transcendent realm. These installations of the good object after individuation – its introjection and transcendent stipulation – are suspended in *communitas*, during which transcendent constructions – the entire structural system of normative separations – collapse.

Reconciled narcissism implies mature group psychology. Alford, continuing the tradition of Kleinian group psychology, distinguishes between "regressed" and "developed" groups. He argues that the former are characterized by the "schizoid compromise," that is, by a recourse to

---

[5] From this perspective individual autonomy seems to derive not only from ownership, as a publicly recognized domain of sovereignty, nor from mature identification alone, but from their combination, that is, from inheritance.

[6] Alongside the imaginary incorporation of a loved object in identification, mature narcissism consists of a narcissistic realm of total, undivided being. This is the realm of omnipotent wholeness that originates in early attachments and which remains indispensable in structure in the forms of myths and traditions. This narcissistic realm is the realm of permanent self-expansion that represents and substitutes total being after individuation-separation has been established. Mature identifications need such a nourishing narcissistic realm to rest on in order to establish and preserve individuation. Mature identifications do not entirely replace primary symbiotic attachments. They depend on the persisting goodness, vitality and wholeness of such attachments and on their narcissistic inputs. Within structures, early life-giving attachments turn into fusion with consoling and empowering concrete traditions of everyday life. Such traditions are superhuman entities with which members of social structures are still fused after individuation takes place. Myths, ideals, traditions and concrete forms of life are extensions of the personality that enable the individual to reach beyond ego-boundaries. Individuating identifications imply firm boundaries and simultaneous expansion into the mythical, archetypal prototypes that are embedded in tradition.

splitting mechanisms in the relationship between individual members and their group. Under the "schizoid compromise" individuals do not participate in social activities as integrated persons among other integrated persons. "This is what group development is, group members spending more time in the middle: neither idealizing nor devaluing the leader, neither isolating themselves from the group nor submerging themselves in it." (Alford 1996, 73) Developed groups are distinguished by the capacity of their members to be "...part of the group and separate from it at the same time, member and individual" (Alford 1996, 70).[7]

Individuals who occupy the reconciled position can dispense of schizoid mechanisms and form, in Alford's terms, a "developed" group. Only they are able to cooperate in social enterprises without risking too much their individuality and separateness. Only they can relate to totemic leadership and hegemony through mature identification, as integrated persons. Alford seems to be right in insisting that developed groups need leaders as much as other groups do; perhaps leaders with whom members can identify as free and complete persons. Still, members of developed groups are marked, according to Alford, by their ability to play some of the leader's roles for themselves instead of projecting them (1996, 68). This ability suggests a mature introjection of parental roles, which characterizes the reconciled position. Occupants of the reconciled position have a relatively vivid and secure social-historical identity, and, indeed, according to Alford, "[d]eveloped groups have a history, a story about the group that connects past, present, and future" (1996, 69).

Occupants of the reconciled position find themselves at home in both

---

[7] According to Alford, group membership and individuality are not in the end fully reconcilable even in developed groups. However, contrary to what Alford's formulations imply, individuality cannot be contrasted with group membership. Individuality is only possible within social structure. It is conditioned by structure's system of objective categories and by other recognized and recognizing individuals. Individuality assumes objectively institutionalized mutual recognition. Alford is right to note that interaction between total human beings is rare, but this does not testify for the fragility of individuality within structure but for its strength. Total interaction characterizes *communitas* rather than structure. Individuation requires that interaction be mediated by normative objective roles. Alford seems to be correct to the extent that (reconciled) membership *threatens* individuality, as latency age phenomena demonstrate. Precisely because the reconciled personality integrates totemic law and identity and does not rest on massive split and projection, defensive regressions of individuality are possible.

private and civic spheres. Contrary to Adorno's critique of reconciliation, their reconciliation to the public sphere does not necessarily imply ego weakness or renunciation of individuality. Under certain circumstances their individuation becomes vulnerable, but ordinarily only they exhibit individuation and integration by virtue of the recognition they enjoy.

The relation between *recognition* and *reconciliation* according to Hegel, and in real life, merits a separate discussion. Suffice it to say that Hegel sometimes seems to consider misrecognition as the cultural form of all social and individual predicament. The totality of each historical mode of being can be described in terms of recognition and misrecognition (Hegel 1977c, 212). Arguably, death becomes the existential problem only as a result of social misrecognition, which excludes a collective "taming of death."[8] Hegel's *Phenomenology* can be interpreted as a survey of the ways in which misrecognition and the consequent lack of reconciliation were in the course of history projected and objectified in dissatisfying representations of the human, the moral, the divine and the natural, that is, in spiritually deprived self-world positions.

Two familiar challenges to the idea of reconciliation will help us specify and qualify its meaning in the present context. First, reconciliation does not imply conformity or conservatism. Many commentators have shown that Hegel's ideal of reconciliation to *ethical life* does not exclude critical speculation (for example, Kaufmann 1970), even if both critical theory and reconciliation are always confined to a historical horizon. Hegel stressed the possibility of criticism explicitly and repeatedly (1942, 3; 1995, 95-96), and such possibility is implicit in his remarks on *reflection* and *speculation* as the forms of ethical thinking. Reconciliation is a general attitude towards the hegemonic-totemic traditions of one's society, an attitude of mature, non-paranoiac identification. In the present discussion, the concept of reconciliation is much slimmer, then, than Nietzsche's concept of *amor fati* (or Schiller's concept of *naive poetry*), which *may* imply an abstinence from criticism, a critical abstinence from criticism. "My formula for greatness in a human being is *amor fati*: that one wants nothing to be different, not forward, not backward, not in all eternity." (Nietzsche 1967b, par. 10) Nietzsche's slightly less radical formulations concerning life assertion, including acceptance of death, may, in fact, often describe aspects of the reconciled position. The reconciled liberal can more easily integrate

---

[8] On the collective 'taming of death' see Aries (1981).

acceptance of death with an assertion of life, on the basis of his mature, non-paranoiac identification with a timeless tradition. He has a better chance of coming to terms with *law* and *enjoyment* (*jouissance*) – as well as death – than occupants of other positions. Because the reconciled person can acknowledge and integrate his own violence, both his own and his Law's violence are mitigated.

Secondly, reconciliation in the present context does not imply a way out of the allegedly tortured and absurd experience of the Other or of others. On the contrary, occupants of the reconciled position live comfortably with the alienation-constant built into every social structure. As we saw, though the forms of alienation from self and others vary across times and places, every social structure, as an order of firm individuation, institutionalizes alienation. Alford, for example, describes an inescapable alienation of individual and group: "There is, it must be recognized, no solution to the problem of individual and group.... Group members never solve the problem of coming to terms with the leader while finding a place for themselves as individuals and members". Alford's "developed groups" rest on a delicate balance between individual and group. They are difficult to maintain, as even they are unable to resolve alienation. Membership in a developed group merely amounts to putting up with alienation. Alford (1996, 120) poignantly criticizes the vision of social harmony conjured up by communitarian proponents of participatory democracy as involving regression of individuality and freedom.

'Reconciliation' in the present discussion is compatible, then, with the reconciled liberal's struggle against glaring social injustice. As a general attitude, reconciliation may coexist with deep-rooted rebelliousness and with forms of alienation.[9] Reconciliation, in the present discussion, does imply a sense of secure membership and a mature, possibly critical, identification with the hegemonic order. It implies acceptance of the general idea of totemic Law, if not of particular legal systems. Reconciliation to the timeless Law involves coming to terms with death and with normative desire (as opposed to *jouissance*). It implies self-knowledge, freedom and integrity within a concrete form of life, a zone of familiarity divided into separate spheres. Occupants of the reconciled position enjoy a relatively secure sense of their own identity and of the identity of others, and their interactional attitudes are less

[9] Hegel's notion of reconciliation is not as thin as the present one (Hardimon 1992).

paranoid. Their ideals and the challenges they undertake are often mainstream ideals prevalent in their society. However, the strong ego of occupants of the reconciled position seems capable of autonomous moral judgement, mutual recognition and compassion. There is a solid sense of the goodness of self without an excessive use of idealization. Strong good self and individuality are reflected in the fact that one does not expect from others, in moral matters, more than one expects from oneself, on the basis of a realistic self-knowledge. A properly individuated person is willing to recognize his personality in its totality and to judge other people in light of the same standards. As we shall see later in this chapter, Adorno criticized even such minimalist accounts of reconciliation, finding them to be conformist and regressive.

In political matters, the reconciled position may find expression in a wide range of ideologies. On the one hand, there is a propensity to support policies which establish universal recognition in the spirit of the *oikos* (household) paradigm. Carl Schmitt (1996, 22-23) asserts that people who entertain an optimistic and charitable conception of human nature tend to be liberals or anarchists. This generalization, subject to a certain psychological reformulation, entails that the reconciled position is essentially liberal. Occupants of the reconciled position, having strong and integrated good selves which nourish optimistic conceptions of human nature, support policies based on trust and the value of universal liberty.

At the same time, self-assertion may incline occupants of the reconciled position towards excessive nationalism (totemic self-assertion) and even towards market libertarianism. Reconciled libertarianism is not as sado-masochistic or vengeful as authoritarian libertarianism – though these motivations still figure in it – but may derive from a Nietzschean life assertion, an assertion of one's power, productivity and freedom. For the reconciled liberal, there is no psychological incentive as strong as that of the alienated liberal to advocate universal principles of welfare and rights. The reconciled person is recognized by the group and does not appeal to universal principles as substitutes for group recognition. However, if universal recognition conditions enduring relationships of mutual recognition, occupants of the reconciled position will be committed to universal principles. Hegel considered mutual recognition to rest upon principles of universal recognition, but these principles may not come to the fore naturally. Habermas writes that the post-conventional self must address itself to an unlimited (universal) communication community in order to establish reflexive self-relation and self-esteem. "A post conventional ego-identity can only stabilize itself in the anticipation of symmetrical relations of unforced reciprocal recognition." (Habermas 1992b, 188) However, only for the alienated liberal does this need in universal recognition become immediate, political, urgent. Habermas seems to neglect the psychoanalytic conditions which spur demands for recognition and universalization.

At the close of his contribution to *The Authoritarian Personality,* Adorno draws a portrait of the "genuine liberal." According to Adorno, the "genuine liberal," as opposed to the authoritarian personality, is characterized by a "balance between superego, ego and id which Freud deemed ideal" (1950, 771). On the whole, the "genuine liberal" is not repressed, and his independent and active ego is "not libidinized – he is rarely narcissistic" (1950, 781). He is compassionate and tends to identify with the underdog. Adorno also attributes to him aesthetic interests and pursuits. If the characteristics listed by Adorno mark anything, it is the threshold of entrance to the reconciled position. These characteristics obtain also in the case of less 'developed' occupants of the reconciled position, who are not yet reconciled *liberals*. These characteristics do not imply an obvious concern for the existence of institutions that embody universal principles of justice.

The more an occupant of the reconciled position is morally developed, the more he will subscribe to principles of universal rights and welfare. This developmental process consists mainly in growing out of the regressive phenomena of latency age. Latency age phenomena are mechanisms of defense in the face of conflicts that follow more or less 'successful' resolutions of the Oedipus complex. They furnish, in fact, some of the best indications for the existence of the Oedipus complex. Oedipal tensions burden and weaken the ego. The reconciled ego, unlike the authoritarian one, is strong. But not too strong. It is leveled, called to order, terrorized. This regimentation eventually turned Adorno against the psychoanalytic ideal of reconciliation, though at first he and his collaborators endorsed Freud's vision of the ideal Oedipus.

As Kernberg illustrates, latency mechanisms are not confined in any way to latency age. "[C]onventional morality, is strikingly similar to the morality of children in the latency phase..." (Kernberg 1995, 164)[10] Some

---

[10] "Latency morality in fact shows great similarity to kitsch – art forms without aesthetic merit but with great popular appeal. Kitsch is usually characterized by sentimentality, obviousness, pretentiousness, grandiosity, the easy simplification of traditionally dominant expressive styles, intellectual superficiality, and the

authors have noted the political implications of primitive latency age morality.

> Conservatism is the state of mind resulting from regression to latency mechanisms in the face of adult responsibility and the depressive task of working through the Oedipus complex and accepting commitment to introjective identification with a combined object. (Meltzer 1973, 154)

The narcissistic wounds and sexual renunciations which allow for resolution of the Oedipus complex precipitate a regression to schizoid mechanisms, such as, split of good and bad, idealization of parents and self, denial, flights to fantasy, superficial identifications and the weakening of ego boundaries.

> The simple morality of the latency age divides individuals and causes into good and bad, dissociates genital sexuality from tender affection and genital sex from polymorphous perverse infantile sexual components, and encourages naivete, a motivated innocence. (Kernberg 1995, 164-65)

Many latency age phenomena would seem familiar to students of authoritarianism. They seem to occur among occupants of the reconciled position during latency age, and then gradually recede, while among authoritarian children they seem to occur at a later stage and to become then permanent.[11] As the authors of *The Authoritarian Personality* found, authoritarian children regress from violence and disobedience to hypocritical and manipulative conformity (Horkheimer 1949, 373), which calls to mind latency fantasies of respectability. Latency age psychology shares with mass psychology and authoritarianism a lack of autonomy along with an avoidance of introspection, excessive idealization of

---

pursuit of childlike ideals: the idealization of what is small, cozy and amusing; images of clowns, a chimney fire against a winter landscape, the warm, protected, safe, simple, and happy environment of (fantasized) childhood. It is this latency-age morality that lends itself to massive projection onto the group and persists throughout adolescence and even into adulthood as a common value system in unstructured groups and under conditions of group repression." (Kernberg 1995, 164-65)

[11] While authoritarian children proceed from deviance to conformity and occupants of the reconciled position progress from conformity to autonomy, future occupants of the alienated position may go through latency without dramatic transformations. While they may not experience debilitating conflicts, they already encounter exclusion from the solidarity of those undergoing latency age conflicts and regressions, the core of future social solidarity.

reference-groups such as the family and the nation, repressed hatred of authority and a resort to all schizoid-paranoid mechanisms. The frustrations of latency often find authoritarian outlets. Kernberg (1995) observes that latency morality reappears as part of mass psychology in the worship of consensus, in hypocritical righteousness and in repression of sexuality. Populism is a form of return to latency age idealization of one's goodness and of human helplessness, as well as latency age aversion to knowledge, science and intellectualism. As Wiles notes, "[p]opulism is anti intellectual. Even its intellectuals try to be anti-intellectual" (1969, 167). Wiles champions a tolerant attitude to populism, perhaps the same tolerance we have towards regressive latency morality.

> Populism is not to be thought of as bad. So widespread a human phenomenon is bound to contain its quota of evil, and certainly this particular one has more than its fair share of the absurd. But particular populist measures are very sound; Tolstoy, Belinski and Cobbett were good people: Bryan, Chernov and Belaunde were democratic politicians in undemocratic periods. (Wiles 1969, 171)

Latency age phenomena suggest that separation and mature identifications have been, to a significant degree, accomplished. The development out of latency age morality consists in the consolidation of separation and autonomy. According to Klein, once separation is reestablished, dependence on schizoid-paranoid mechanisms and latency morality is reduced. At a certain point, the process of separation becomes a process of *abstraction* of personal identity, as well. Once a certain level of separation is achieved, the self can replace and multiply the external objects to which it is attached and turn to more distant and abstract objects.

This personal process is augmented by a historical process of abstraction of ego identities. The transition from *mechanic* to *organic* solidarity, to use Durkheim's terms, involves the formation and public recognition of a rich variety of personal identities. Habermas describes this historical development of the life-world in terms of processes of rationalization, differentiation and individuation. "[P]rocesses of societal differentiation... have set in motion a generalization of values and, especially in the system of rights, a universalization of norms, and these processes demand a specific kind of independent accomplishment from the socialized individuals. The onus of these decisions requires a nonconventional ego-identity." (Habermas 1992b, 187) Thus, women's moral development, for example, depended, according to Gilligan, on the social recognition of their autonomy.

> [T]he concept of rights changes women's conceptions of self, allowing them to see themselves as stronger and to consider directly their own needs... changes in women's rights change women's moral judgements, seasoning mercy with justice... (Gilligan 1982, 149)

The personal and social processes of abstraction are enhanced by a peaceful exposure to a variety of forms of life. Gadamer argues that in the course of hermeneutic encounters with other cultures horizons are continuously universalized (Gadamer 1975, 271-73). Abstraction and cultivation of individuality can also be traced to experiences of struggle and suffering. The romantic idealization of the efforts of *Bildung* is echoed throughout Hegel's philosophy, where it is elevated to the status of a meta-historical concept. The questioning of the familiar is a painful process: "The road can therefore be regarded as the pathway of *doubt*, or more precisely as the way of despair." (1977c, 49) Self-knowledge originates in the dissolution of familiar and harmonious *ethical life*.

> Thus when philosophy is to emerge among a people, there must first have been a break in the real world. At that point philosophy is the reconciliation of the corruption which had been begun by thought. This reconciliation happens in the ideal world, in the world of the spirit into which men take flight when the earthly world satisfies them no longer. (Hegel 1985, 113)[12]

---

[12] *See also* Hegel (1942) 138R. Gadamer writes in a similar vein: "Tradition, part of whose nature is the handing-on of traditional material, must have become questionable for an explicit consciousness of the hermeneutic task of appropriating tradition to have been formed" (1975, xxi); "...hermeneutics came to flower in the Romantic era as a consequence of the modern dissolution of firm bonds with tradition" (1976, 21). Spirit progresses through struggle: "...the stage of self consciousness [spirit] has reached is the principle which it reveals in history in the relations of that existence. This principle it clothes with all the wealth of its existence; the shape in which it exists is a people into whose morality, constitution, domestic, civil, and public life, arts, international relations, etc. this principle is built... This is the material which the principle of a people has to work through... This is a progress not in empty time but in time infinitely filled and full of struggle; on the contrary, this material only advances in pure thinking *pair pass* with its advance in its entire concrete life." (Hegel 1985, 44) Like Hegel, Nietzsche (1967a, II 1-3) compared the Greek mode of being to childhood innocence, and conceived of successive processes of cultivation as inevitably painful and violent.

Social conflicts, conflicts between desires and commitments and between different commitments are said to foster, then, individual development. Carol Gilligan describes how through the experience of crises and conflicts of commitments women abstract concrete commitments into general principles and establish a sense of individuality and self-worth. The conflict of commitments in cases of abortion, for instance, drives women to subject their concrete commitments to critical examination.

> The abortion study suggests that women impose a distinctive construction on moral problems, seeing moral dilemmas in terms of conflicting responsibilities. This construction was traced through a sequence of three perspectives, each perspective representing a more complex understanding of the relationship between self and other and each transition involving a critical reinterpretation of the conflict between selfishness and responsibility. The sequence of women's moral judgment proceeds from an initial concern with survival to a focus on goodness and finally to a reflective understanding of care as the most adequate guide to the resolution of conflicts in human relationships... (Gilligan 1982, 105)

Gilligan distinguishes between two general moral imperatives:

> The moral imperative that emerges repeatedly in interviews with women is an injunction to care, a responsibility to discern and alleviate the 'real and unrecognizable trouble' of this world. For men, the moral imperative appears rather as an injunction to respect the rights of others and thus to protect from interference the rights to life and self-fulfillment. Women's insistence on care is at first self-critical rather than self protective, while men initially conceive obligation to others negatively in terms of non interference. (Gilligan 1982, 100)

While men conceive of moral dilemmas as arising from conflicts between rules that regulate and coordinate individual egoistic efforts, women see "moral dilemmas in terms of conflicting responsibilities" (Gilligan 1982, 105). According to Gilligan, an ethics of care is rooted in a stronger sense of human interdependence, perhaps interdependence as the essential setting for self-realization rather than a fact with which we have to put up. The claims issued by an ethics of care are constituted by particular personal relationships in which we are involved. Even if women's conceptualization of ethical commitments and dilemmas can be traced to the continuous female attachment to the maternal sphere, it is wrong to stipulate a dichotomy between male and female ethics. Gilligan's theoretical interpretation of her findings is too simplistic. Her findings only support the conclusion that in the separation-abstraction process women's starting point – probably in both the maternal and paternal spheres – is one of greater attachment. Her dichotomous theoretical construction seems to be contradicted by a variety of familiar counter-examples. There are men who, for example, conceptualize moral problems as conflicts of concrete commitments in the private sphere. Care is an important component in the ethical sensitivity of men, though it is perhaps more easily universalized by them, at least if they are reconciled or alienated liberals. Furthermore, many men find it difficult to internalize and apply social rules and principles, especially if they are authoritarian or alienated. A parallel variety of combinations can be observed among women.

The separation-abstraction process turns the hypocrisy and conformity of latency age and mass psychology into a post-conventional critical attitude. It is then realized that "good men must not obey the laws too well" (Emerson 1983, 563) and that "...it is not right that honourable men should be the executioners of others" (Cervantes 1950, 178). Abstraction of one's concrete commitments leads to a universal concern for individual welfare and freedom. Gilligan describes insightfully the process of the universalization of care:

> [T]he focus shifts to the consideration of what constitutes care... Care then becomes a universal injunction, a self chosen ethic which freed from its conventional interpretation, leads to a recasting of the dilemma in a way that allows the assumption of responsibility for choice. (Gilligan 1982, 90)

According to Gilligan (1982, 94), the universalization of care is related to the emergence of a separate good and worthy self, capable of autonomous post-conventional choices and recognition of a realm of the right.

The preceding integrative – if not eclectic – approach to moral development differs from Kohlberg's approach. First, the moral-developmental process is seen as conditioned by one's position. Not everybody undergoes the developmental process from conformity to autonomy, or from a "constitutional" to an "overlapping" consensus, to use Rawls' terms. This process assumes a certain constellation of recognition-relations, namely, those characteristic of the reconciled position. Indeed, as Kohlberg expects from morally developed persons, reconciled liberals subscribe to Rawlsian ideals. The reconciled person subscribes to Rawls's interpretation of fairness and will be more "reasonable" than occupants of other positions in the Rawlsian sense of "reasonableness", as the willingness to bracket controversial "comprehensive doctrines" in order to facilitate fair, all embracing social cooperation. The authoritarian personality seems to be stuck in Kohlberg's first stage. Unable to internalize norms, it abides by them ostensibly in order to gain entrance into respectable society (pseudoconservatism). Alienated liberals often seem to begin from Kohlberg's highest, critical stage and then, occasionally, draw closer to traditional social conventions. A second criticism of Kohlberg is that the developmental process itself is not predominantly a pragmatic, cognitive learning process. It has more to do with working through latency age morality, relations to parents, attitudes to sexuality and so on. The development from conformity to autonomy cannot be detached from general psychoanalytic and existential processes.

Kohlberg's conception of the substantial moral destination of the developmental process is convincing. The reconciled liberal would support welfare policy in accordance with the household paradigm – i.e., the Rawlsian view of society as a fair system of cooperation – which underlies a developed sense of justice. The reconciled liberal reconciles fairness with self-assertion. The authoritarian personality would typically oppose welfare policy out of its preference for policies of misrecognition, its lack of empathy and its sado-masochistic relation to power. Money and the market become Absolute Masters, masochistically admired for their arbitrary determination of individual fates. The authoritarian personality asserts civil society against the state – the epitome of maternal structure – which it deeply resents and envies. The abstract categories of civil society, such as alienated labor, are asserted over concrete and integrated forms of life reflective of firm attachments. Fascist commitments to welfare are usually merely rhetorical and opportunistic. In the case of alienated liberalism, egalitarianism is defensive. The alienated liberal strives to anchor universal recognition in constitutional principles as substitutes for the social recognition of which he is deprived.

The relationship of the reconciled personality to *democracy* is complicated.[13] The reconciled liberal may be reconciled to an

---

[13] Even though the present model applies to modern societies and democracy is arguably constitutive of modern political systems, we should exercise our imagination and confront occupants of the three positions also with old and utopian political institutions. It cannot be assumed that the model is valid only for

undemocratic society. Similarly, the "democratic" character-types Lasswell and Winnicott describe and praise may well be just as politically content under an enlightened monarchy, for example. Lasswell (1951) depicts the democratic self as characterized by confidence in human nature, openness and pluralism. However, these characteristics do not necessarily correspond to democratic convictions. Nor are the virtues of "democratic community" that Lasswell enumerates restricted to democracies. Winnicott contrasts the democratic character with various kinds of "anti-social" personalities, but nowhere does he explain why "democratic personalities," having enjoyed proper maternal care and being "grown-up enough not to mind playing at being children" (Winnicott 1965, 165), would be committed exclusively to democracy. The same is true of Fromm's account of democratic commitment. Fromm was interested in the psychological basis of democratic commitment that secures aversion and resistance to fascism. This is easily understandable in light of the political circumstances that stimulated Fromm's investigations. However, the anti-fascist personality would not be committed exclusively to democracy, but to other possible non-fascist régimes as well.[14]

The trust and openness which distinguish occupants of the reconciled position from the other two positions do not have to be translated into democratic principles. While reconciled trust implies an initial inclination to believe in the judgement and goodness of the common people, it also implies a non-paranoiac relation to authority, whether democratic or not democratic. Hegel and Aristotle described the threats democratic political equality and struggle for power pose to social structure,[15] precious to the reconciled liberal. Democracy, according to Hegel, champions popular virtue at the expense of institutional structure. Hegel, as we shall see in the next section, captures the populist moment of democracy in its 'sentimental' belief in common goodness and in its anti-structural tendencies.[16] While undeveloped, populist reconciliation might be

---

a specific form of political organization, namely, democracy.

[14] Fromm (1984) studied the relation between left-wing ideology and democratic commitment empirically.

[15] Aristotle *The Politics* (1995) books V, VI.

[16] Nietzsche, too, perceives the conflict between democracy and structure and the necessity to counterbalance democracy in order to protect the institutions of social structure: "Democracy has always been the declining form of the power to

expressed in endorsement of democratic language, developed reconciliation would entail support for democracy, as a tradition of fair decision-making and compromise,[17] only as long as it does not threaten structure and individuation. It seems that in many ways the reconciled liberal's attitude to democracy would resemble Tocqueville's ambiguous attitude. Democracy would seem to the reconciled liberal fair and at the same time a potential source of dangers, such as, decline of individuality and structure and tyranny of conformist public opinion.

Hegelian Ideas on Reconciled Politics

In the remaining sections of this chapter, the foregoing outline of the reconciled position will be extended through discussion of some Hegelian and psychoanalytic concepts. After a discussion of Hegel's own ideas, their sublation in the works of G.H. Mead will be considered, without doing justice to the wealth and depth of Mead's insights into political psychology. Finally, the familiar claim that resolution of the Oedipus complex underlies socialization will be invoked in order to flesh out the concept of reconciliation in terms of classical psychoanalytic theory. As in the case of authoritarianism, a psychoanalytic understanding of political reconciliation will require application of Kleinian concepts in addition to the Freudian concepts of the Frankfurt School.

While current conceptions of the 'psychological' and the 'existential' differ from those prevalent in Hegel's days, Hegel's ideas remain indispensable for the political psychologist. Hegel devised insightful accounts of historical value-systems that can be translated into psychological and existential terms. The *Phenomenology of Spirit* sets in motion a glorious procession of perceptively portrayed ethical characters. Out of the wealth of ethical-psychological characters and processes Hegel describes, we will focus our attention on his accounts of revolutionary terror and post-revolutionary reconciliation with modern *ethical life*. This

---

organize... For institutions to exist there must exist the kind of will, instinct, imperative which is anti-liberal to the point of malice: the will to tradition, to authority, to centuries-long responsibility, to solidarity between succeeding generations backwards and forwards in infinitum"; Fragment 39 in "Expeditions of an untimely man" in *Twilight of the Idols* (Nietzsche, 1968a, 93).

[17] On fairness in democracy see Singer (1973, 32ff.). The reconciled liberal's attitude to democracy has to do with his general attitude to fairness.

distinction between alienated and reconciled liberalism structures the present model along with other Hegelian concepts, such as, recognition and differentiated spheres of interaction. Hegel criticized the ideals of the Enlightenment and the French Revolution insofar as they advocated complete independence from traditional institutions of *ethical life* and appealed instead to empty universality. This perceptive Hegelian approach to alienated liberalism will be discussed in the next chapter.[18]

Reconciled values are held by the reconciled citizens envisaged in Hegel's theory of the modern state. Hegel's account of these values, as expressing the *concretely embodied* universality of the state and its citizens, is essential to our understanding of political reconciliation. Hegel's account complements the classical psychoanalytic perspective in suggesting that reconciliation reflects individual acceptance of a *historically concrete ethical life* that aspires to institutionalize *universal* recognition. Citizens of the Hegelian state who identify with its historical (and universal) institutions – that is, recognize themselves in these institutions – are reconciled liberals. Their reconciliation to modern *ethical life* amounts to reconciliation to – and between – all spheres of interaction. The citizen of the Hegelian state would abide by its liberal institutions from a recognized and reconciled position.[19]

---

[18] 'Alienation' here is understood in its loose everyday sense, not necessarily in accordance with Hegel's accounts in *The Phenomenology of Spirit* of the alienation of "the unhappy consciousness" and "self-estranged spirit".

[19] Occupants of the reconciled position are not necessarily reconciled *liberals*. They become liberals only if they undergo a development out of latency age morality. In Hegel's terms, the development from particularity to universality is a development from 'reflection' to 'speculation'. Reason emerges out of praxis, development is brought about through everyday struggle in the midst of *ethical life*. The individual gradually emerges out of social substance and comes to *speculate* about it critically. *Reflection* defines individuals as it defines everything: by drawing contrasts and interpersonal distinctions. "Self-development means asserting itself, entering existence, becoming something different... the developing thing acquires existence in relation to other things, in difference from them..." (Hegel 1985, 73) Therefore, self-reflection produces atomistic self-understanding (Hegel 1942, 256R) and self-assertion. These find expression in war and civil society. Mutual recognition is the achievement of speculation. Speculation dissolves the oppositions constructed by reflection (Hegel 1977a, 99, 113). But the universality attained by speculation is concretely embodied. The separation-abstraction process – the reconciled person's developmental path Kohlberg described – leads towards concretely

Some would argue, though not as many as a few years ago, that Hegel's political philosophy is far from liberal, and that its psychological foundations cannot illuminate the political psychology of liberalism. Hegel's statements about democracy and war, as well as his theory of punishment (Hegel 1942, 100, 101, 273R, 324R, 324A), are an anathema to many liberals. Yet his conception of recognition and universality in the state, his advocacy of the imposition of constraints on civil society and his aversion to any form of nationalist irrationalism in politics, shed light on the psychological basis of liberal politics. Allen Wood quotes Cousin's remark that "[Hegel was] infused with the new spirit; he considered the French Revolution to be the greatest step forward taken by humankind since Christianity. He was profoundly liberal without being the least bit republican" (Wood 1990, 257). Wood concedes that institutions of the Hegelian state are liberal but argues that Hegel's theoretical justification of these institutions departs from liberalism in that it does not proceed from an atomistic conception of human nature (1990, 258-59). However, this does not separate Hegel from contemporary liberalism, which by and large discards the atomistic conceptions of classical liberalism. Wood argues further that Hegel departs from liberalism in insisting that the state serves collective goals and does not confine itself to facilitating individual interests. It is arguable that liberalism can accommodate the idea of collective goals, too. Collective goals, according to Hegel, as Wood admits, do not conflict with individual goals, and a *liberal ethical life* is the supreme collective goal.[20]

Hegel's basic conception of reconciled individuality, situated in the midst of *concrete ethical life* on the basis of *universal* recognition, underlies his critique of the Revolution and his account of the modern state. *Individuality*, as a *concrete* identity that is an organ of a *universal* order, emerges through universal recognition. Through universal recognition the reconciled liberal becomes reconciled to his concrete identity as an organ of a universal order.[21] Mutual recognition assumes a universal perspective: the standpoint of the state, the whole. The

---

embodied, rather than abstract, universality.

[20] The literature on the relations between Hegel and liberalism is enormous and constantly growing. See, for example, Taylor (1991).

[21] O'Neill (1996) is a good collection of articles on the dialectics of mutual recognition.

universal principles embodied in the state objectify the universal standpoint that validates recognition. Alongside universality, individuality involves concrete, differentiated identity, rooted in a concrete historical tradition. As soon as revolutionary turmoil weakened, old traditions that had provided people with concrete differentiated identities had to be restored.

> These individuals who have felt the fear of death, of their absolute master, again submit to negation and distinctions, arrange themselves in the various spheres, and return to an apportioned and limited task, but thereby to their substantial reality. (Hegel 1977c, 361)

Freedom consists in knowing, and being reconciled to one's concrete identity in an *ethical life* whose participants universally recognize each other's concrete identity. According to Hegel, only in the modern (liberal) state such freedom is realizable. Universal self-realization is constitutive of the modern state, in whose institutions (almost) all individuals find their human image charitably reflected. The reconciliation of the individual to the modern state is conditioned by the state's continuing adherence to the *values of reconciled liberalism*, which are built into the very structure of its institutions. According to Hegel, the principle of the state is *unity of the particular and the universal.* The state, as opposed to civil society, is the sphere in which the interests of the individual coincide with the interest of the whole (Hegel 1942, 181, 184, 186, 236, 257, 258R, 260, 261R, 263R, 264). Political obligation is, then, in accord with personal freedom. "In the state as something ethical, as the inter-penetration of the substantive and the particular, my obligation to what is substantive is at the same time the embodiment of my particular freedom." (Hegel 1942, 261R)

This identity of the universal and particular is achieved when individuals can realize themselves as members of a state in their full particularity. Moreover, this is the only way for individuals fully to realize themselves.

> Since the state is mind objectified, it is only as one of its members that the individual himself has objectivity, genuine individuality, and an ethical-life. (Hegel 1942, 258R)

> ... since he possesses as a citizen the self-conscious power of universality, he thereby acquires the right of desire and, at the same time, preserves his freedom in regard to it. (Hegel 1977c, 274)

The abstraction of civil society – its misrecognition of the differentiated, concretely-embodied identity – is overcome by universal recognition of each individual in his particularity in other spheres of *ethical life*.[22] Real recognition allows for no abstraction. Universal recognition is realized through differentiation of interrelated concrete positions that form a rational, universal whole.

> A man actualizes himself only in becoming something definite, i.e. something specifically particularized; this means restricting himself exclusively to one of the particular spheres of need. (Hegel 1942, 207)

> The principle of modern states has prodigious strength and depth because it allows the principle of subjectivity to progress to its culmination in the extreme of self-subsistent personal particularity, and yet at the same time brings it back to the substantive unity and so maintains this unity in the principle of subjectivity itself. (Hegel 1942, 260) [23]

The unity of universal and particular in the state requires the actual well-being of all individuals. It requires that each individual have the material conditions for self-realization.

> The essence of the modern state is that the universal be bound up with the complete freedom of its particular members and with private well-being... (Hegel 1942, 260A)

> Welfare without right is not a good. Similarly, right without welfare is not the good; *fiat justitia* should not be followed by *pereat mundus.* (Hegel 1942, 130)

Hegel's, *as well as other versions of reconciled liberalism*, do not, however, require formal equality, which is a form of abstract misrecognition.

> The demand sometimes made for an equal division of land, and other

---

[22] See *Phenomenology of Spirit* (1977c, 213-14) for a description of universal recognition as embodied in *ethical life*.

[23] The universality of the state makes possible the realization of individuality since, according to Hegel, individuality and particularity must always be mediated by universality, and this universal essence is realized in social recognition. Individuality comes into being through social recognition. "Self-consciousness exists in and for itself when, and by the fact that, it so exists for another; that is, it exists only in being acknowledged." (1977c, 111) It depends on the existence of social institutions that recognize subjectivity and autonomy.

> available resources too, is an intellectualism all the more empty and superficial in that at the heart of particular differences there lies not only the external contingency of nature but also the whole compass of mind, endlessly particularized and differentiated, and the rationality of mind developed into an organism. (Hegel 1942, 49R)[24]

Hegel understood that the state he portrayed cannot put up with poverty. Poverty constitutes a real threat to the state.

> The state is actual only when its members have a feeling of their own self-good and it is stable only when public and private ends are identical. It has often been said that the end of the state is the happiness of the citizens. That is perfectly true. If all is not well with them, if their subjective aims are not satisfied, if they do not find that the state as such is the means to their satisfaction, then the footing of the state itself is insecure. (Hegel 1942, 265A)[25]

According to Hegel's, and other versions of reconciled liberalism, even if civil society must be constrained it remains a condition for the *freedom* and *reconciliation* of the modern citizen. Civil society, as the domain of the "particular," is the sphere in which an a-historical aspect of freedom is realized. According to Ritter (1982, 65), the rupture between modern man and tradition, as seen by Hegel, will never be completely remedied and is perpetuated through the institutionalization of civil society. Civil society establishes a sphere of self-assertion in which

---

[24] Drydyk (1991) argues that Hegel would have sided with moderate socialism under which state and civil society coexist without encroaching too much upon each other. In Dworkin's terms, the Hegelian reconciled liberal would advocate equality of resources rather than equality of welfare.

[25] Furthermore, Hegel thought that the state cannot justify its legitimacy in the eyes of the poor. In a controversial passage from Hegel's lectures of 1819-1820 on the Philosophy of Right, Hegel argues that poverty undermines the rational substance of the state, in which the justification of punishment is grounded. There is no *right* to punish the poor: "Earlier we had seen the right of distress as relating to a momentary necessity. Here necessity no longer has this purely momentary character. In the emergence of poverty the power of particularity comes to existence against the reality of the free. Herein is the basis leading to the infinite judgement of the criminal. The crime can well be punished, but this punishment is contingent." Translated by Tunick (1992, 140-41) from Hegel (1983, 195-96). Poverty cannot be completely eliminated but the state should strive to diminish it as much as possible (Hegel 1942, 245). For an exposition of this Hegelian conception of poverty see Avineri (1972, 147-54).

tradition is neutralized. The abstract reason of the Revolution is reconciled to existing *ethical life* only through the inclusion of civil society in *ethical life*. The reconciled liberal will not shun the objectification of some of his freedom in civil society, yet demand its restriction.

Construed in a Hegelian vein, reconciled liberalism would be suspicious of democracy. Democracy is not a condition for free, uncoerced and reconciled citizenship. Democracy can turn into the worst tyranny, as it did in the course of the French Revolution. Like the ideal of formal equality, democracy poses a threat to the differentiation of individual identities. According to Hegel, democracy is a sentimental social order based on the assumption of universal, political vocation and popular inner virtue. Reason and individual self-realization require the division of society into different classes, each with different responsibilities. Such a division provides every individual with a determinate identity. Political vocation is not universal. According to Hegel, the executive class is responsible for running the state (Hegel 1942, 294R, 297, 297A). In democracy, identities are ambiguous and citizens do not know themselves, partly because they are at once subjects and rulers.

> Taken without its monarch and the articulation of the whole which is the indispensable and direct concomitant of monarchy, the people is a formless mass and no longer a state. It lacks every one of those determinate characteristics – sovereignty, government, judges, magistrates, class-divisions, etc., – which are to be found only in a whole which is inwardly organized. (Hegel 1942, 273)

Hegel describes democracy as a "formless mass" because democratic principles of equality undermine the objective categories that constitute social structure as a system of differences. Democratic principles of equality assume abstract individuals, devoid of objectively anchored, concrete identities. Hegel's critique of democracy sheds light on the constitution of the reconciled and alienated positions. Both reconciled and alienated liberals would oppose authoritarian attempts to realize the idea of popular sovereignty word for word. Taken literally, democracy threatens social structure, often in response to authoritarian motivations. Reconciled and alienated liberals would support only a democratic régime that maintains structure, for example, by the reproduction of elites and institutions and an independent judiciary that is not an agent of public opinion.

Mead: Self-Assertion and Mutual Recognition in Liberalism

Mead offers another theoretical conceptualization of the relation between recognition and features of the reconciled position. Following Hegel, Mead (1934, 195, 204) linked the dialectics of recognition with the emergence of self-consciousness. Self-consciousness is a consciousness of one's *Me* (1934, 174-77), which Mead distinguishes from one's *I*. It is the *Me* of each individual that is *recognized* by others and that is socially defined (1934, 214). At the same time, the *I* constantly seeks self-assertion, self-expression and superiority (1934, 205-9). Language is the source and medium of mutual recognition, because it is inherently oriented towards action based on rational consensus (1934, 149). Communication, properly understood, "calls out in the individual himself the tendency to the same act that is called out in others" (1934, 328). Furthermore, an element of universality enters the picture since "[u]niversal discourse is the formal ideal of communication" (1934, 327).[26] Full, mature individuation requires the institutionalization of universal recognition.

It has been noted in the previous section how institutions of the Hegelian state objectify universal recognition. Mead subjects social institutions to similar psychological considerations, yet, at times, reaches different conclusions. For example, Mead was a staunch democrat (1934, 327). In democracy and other cooperative activities, he suggested, people achieve a fusion of mutual recognition and self-assertion. Mead would have characterized the reconciled liberal as exhibiting the ideal psychological constitution: the right balance between mutual recognition and self-assertion. This is a balance between the *I* and the *Me*, which results from proper socialization.

A harmonious balance of *I* and *Me* can be achieved in different spheres of life in spite of the ongoing conflict between them. Mead regarded teamwork as an example of a successful *fusion* of *I* and *Me* (1934, 277). In his paper on "The Psychology of Punitive Justice," Mead explains this phenomenon:

---

[26] These ideas were borrowed by Habermas and served as the foundation of his general theory of communicative action and his discourse-ethics (Habermas 1990a).

> Through rivalries, competitions, and cooperations men achieved the conception of a social state in which they asserted themselves while they at the same time affirmed the status of the others, on the basis not only of common rights and privileges but also on the basis of differences of interest and function in an organization of more varied individuals. In the modern economic world a man is able to assert himself much more effectively against others through his acknowledgement of common property rights underlying their whole economic activity; while he demands acknowledgement for his individual competitive effort by recognizing and utilizing the carried activities and economic functions of others in the whole business complex. (1964, 229)

Mead's description of the fusion of *I* and *Me* captures much of the essence of the state of reconciliation. The fusion achieved in cooperative activity and in religious experience amounts to reconciliation with society and the world, at least within certain fields of action. To be sure, even though liberal universality is a formal ideal implicit in every *Me*, the *I* and the *Me* can reach an apparently prosperous balance in attitudes that are inherently antagonistic to liberalism. For example, "[t]he mob furnishes a situation in which the Me is one which simply supports and emphasizes the more violent sort of impulsive expression... The situation in which one can let himself go, in which the very structure of the Me opens the door for the I, is favourable to self-expression" (1934, 213). The fusion of *I* and *Me* is desirable only when the subjects and objects of self-assertion and mutual recognition are differentiated, integrated individuals. Mead relates the formation of liberal attitudes to the emergence of functional differentiation. Functional differentiation, according to Mead, allows for ample self-assertion and contains an inbuilt moment of mutual recognition.

> What is involved in the development of a universal society is just such a functional organization as we find in economic development… One may say that the attainment of... functional differentiation and social participation in the full degree is a sort of ideal which lies before the human community... the implication of democracy is rather that the individual can be as highly developed as lies within the possibilities of his own inheritance, and still can enter into the attitudes of others whom he affects. (1934, 287, 326) [27]

---

[27] Mead's ideas about functional differentiation are reminiscent of Durkheim's theory of the transition from mechanic to organic solidarity and the concomitant *transformation of morality*. "Just as social similarities give rise to a law and a

Mead, in fact, insists on the need to preserve media for individual self-assertion in a society for its members to be capable of genuine mutual-recognition. Under functional differentiation, self-assertion, together with interdependence and common effort, produce social fraternity and concern.

> The development of the democratic community implies the removal of castes as essential to the personality of the individual; the individual is not to be what he is in his specific caste or group set over against other groups, but his distinctions are to be distinctions of functional difference which put him in relationship with others instead of separating him. (1934, 318)[28]

In his paper on the "Psychology of Punitive Justice," Mead contrasts the "attitude of hostility" of "the self which responds to the call of the community" with the "reconstructive attitude" of the "effective self" (1964, 234). The former, reminiscent of authoritarianism, is backward looking and oriented towards stigmatization and revenge rather than towards understanding. The hostile self is not autonomous since "[j]ust in proportion as we organize by hostility do we suppress individuality" (1964, 228, 223). Furthermore, the hostile self's evaluative judgements, like those of "slave morality" according to Nietzsche, are essentially negations of the other.

> The type of valuation of social goods that arises out of the hostile attitude toward the criminal is negative, because it does not present the positive social function of the goods that the hostile procedure protects. (1964, 224)

The non-hostile attitude, oriented towards understanding and social progress, is forward-looking. Mead boldly states that "... the two attitudes, that of control of crime by the hostile procedure of the law and that of control through comprehension of social and psychological conditions, cannot be combined" (1964, 228, 232). The latter attitude is grounded in a balance between mutual recognition and individual

---

morality that protect them, so the division of labour gives rise to rules ensuring peaceful and regular co-operation between the functions that have been divided up." (Durkheim 1984, 338)

[28] This fraternity makes possible democratic attitudes: "...democracy, in the sense here relevant, is an attitude which depends upon the type of self which goes with the universal relations of brotherhood, however that be reached." (Mead 1934, 286)

self-assertion (1964, 229). This rational, pragmatic and constructive attitude of the non-hostile self derives directly from the mutual recognition of different individuals engaged in the pursuit of shared ideals. It is a reconciled attitude.[29] Mead's reconstructive, forward-looking self supports lenient sentencing policy, welfare policies and cosmopolitanism.[30] Mead offers insightful descriptions of the reconciled, constructive attitude and its manifestations in relation to a range of moral and political issues. While his interpretation of this attitude reflects prejudices of his own time and place – the economic ideals of the nineteenth century and the specifically American vision of democracy – it does capture the structure of a socio-psychological process which fosters the emergence and exercise of reconciled liberal dispositions.

Reconciliation from a Psychoanalytic Perspective

In classical psychoanalytic doctrine the Oedipus complex is seen as the key to the internalization of norms and roles and to socialization in general, i.e., to social *reconciliation*. According to Freud, successful resolution of the Oedipus complex involves a differentiated identification with the two spheres. This complex identification is a condition for social reconciliation and is characteristic of occupants of the reconciled position. As we saw earlier, latency age phenomena precipitated by a successful resolution of the Oedipus complex are most typical of the reconciled position. However, as most contemporary theorists recognize, the Freudian account of Oedipal identification and reconciliation cannot be endorsed as it stands.

Contrary to his own earlier position, Adorno (1968) ridiculed the psychoanalytic glorification of the super-ego and of the integrated "genital personality" in general.[31] In *The Ego and the Id*, Freud describes the boy's identification with and introjection of the father in the form of

---

[29] The alienated liberal's attitude to crime would probably be similar.

[30] See Mead's essays "Philanthropy from the Point of View of Ethics" (1964, 392-407) and "National-Mindedness and International-Mindedness" (1964, 355-70).

[31] For the early position, see *The Authoritarian Personality* (Adorno *et al.* 1950, 771).

the super-ego as a narcissistic desexualization that wins the support and cooperation of the id. This maneuver is meant to repress the Oedipus complex, a task particularly suited for the introjected father figure (Freud 1923a, 33-35). The formation of the super-ego rests, then, on collusion with the id: a narcissistic regression, a surrender to social pressures at the expense of emancipatory consciousness. Adorno criticizes the all too easy compromise of psychoanalytic theory with the super-ego's conventional and regressive nature: "...it is a mockery of the analytic principle to tolerate irrationalities merely because they stem from society and because an organized society is supposedly unthinkable without them..." (Adorno 1968, 82)

Adorno goes on to criticize explicitly the psychoanalytic ideal of *reconciliation*:

> The goal of the 'well-integrated personality' is objectionable because it expects the individual to establish an equilibrium between conflicting forces which does not obtain in existing society - nor should it, because those forces are not of equal moral merit. People are taught to forget the objective conflicts which necessarily repeat themselves in every individual, instead of being helped to grapple with them. The well-balanced person who no longer sensed the inner conflict of psychological forces, the irreconcilable claims of id and ego, would not thereby have achieved an inner resolution of social conflicts. He would be confusing his psychic state – his personal good fortune – with objective reality. His integration would be a false reconciliation with an unreconciled world, and would presumably amount in the last analysis to an 'identification with the aggressor', a mere character mask of subordination. (Adorno 1968, 83)

On the one hand, there is some truth in Adorno's moral critique of what he takes to be the psychoanalytic conception of reconciliation. Post-Oedipal reconciliation does imply an initial motivation to conform – captured, perhaps, by Kohlberg's concept of the "conventional stage" – and, in that respect, Adorno's criticism is correct. On the other hand, the post-Oedipal reconciliation in question is not, strictly speaking, moral reconciliation. It is compatible in the long run with radical moral disapproval, so that Adorno's criticism is somewhat irrelevant. The social reconciliation produced by resolution of the Oedipus complex does not imply acceptance of existing injustice. Furthermore, Adorno's moral criticism may be not only irrelevant, but also wrong. Freudians argue that initial conformity is a *condition* for mature autonomy. The Freudian super-ego can, as Freud believed, foster individual responsibility and facilitate the establishment of firm individual boundaries and autonomy in the face of group regression. The super-ego can facilitate the formation of a secure ethical identity and ethical knowledge, as knowledge of one's roles and obligations. The post-Oedipal super-ego testifies for acceptance of painful renunciations and of one's subjection to rules. Such conformity has positive aspects. It goes hand in hand with renunciation of longings for self-expansion to which authoritarian ideology responds.

Nonetheless, Freud's account is deficient in that it failed to observe the *pre-Oedipal* roots of these ethical achievements, as well as additional advantages of a non-authoritarian institution of the super-ego. Klein's theory shows us how resolutions of the Oedipus complex generally enable non-paranoiac, rich and trust-based object relations. Whereas Freud's psychology implies a conception of post-Oedipal guilt as the essence of ethics and morality, Klein's theory assumes a much wider conception of value. From a Kleinian perspective, non-authoritarian super-ego testifies for the structural dominance of the good self, trust and mature object relations. Morality cannot be reduced to introjected paternal commands, and guilt – to their violation. Moral judgements reflect above all the overall structure of the object-world. One's most basic senses of goodness and badness are built into the object-world. The extent and nature of the internalization of social norms (Freudian super-ego) depend on the structure of the object-world, i.e., on whether the good or bad self, good or bad objects, are dominant, and on whether one's objects of identification support or assault the ego. The ethical standards legislated by agents of socialization with which we identify are superimposed onto an already existing object-world that involves general evaluations of oneself and others, of goodness and badness. Klein elucidates the basic, rudimentary, meaning of goodness and badness that antedates guilt: goodness and badness of the self, of the object and of the object relation, goodness and badness as pleasure and pain, love and hate. The very structure of the ego and the object-world is permeated with and partly shaped by basic evaluations which underlie all future object relations and ethical judgements and concerns. The object-world, as a system of identifications, is shaped by early relations of recognition and misrecognition. A mature, well established super-ego already assumes an entire system of supporting values and identifications, firm and consistent recognition, a rich matrix of reliable relationships. Freud did not sufficiently relate the super-ego to the totality of interpersonal relationships and narrowed down morality to the field of the post-Oedipal, exacting super-ego, an isolated introjection of rational paternal authority.

Moreover, Klein offers important revisions of Freud's moral psychology which remain *within* the theory of guilt and the super-ego. Klein broadens Freud's view of the super-ego. The father is no longer seen as the sole source of the super-ego. The mother makes at least an equal contribution. Furthermore, according to Klein, the super-ego is not only harsh and exacting but is also the source of self love, a sort of fusion of Freud's super-ego and ego ideal.[32] The roots of the integrated super-ego are early internal objects that propel the ego into a massive use of schizoid mechanisms. "These two aspects of the mother's breast are introjected and form the core of the super-ego." (Klein 1952, 70) Klein's understanding of guilt, like her understanding of ethics in general and of the super-ego, is wider than Freud's. Even though Freud (1930) acknowledges the existence of guilt before the super-ego, he conceives of guilt as the inner voice of command on the occasion of transgression. For Klein, guilt is much more basic. It is inseparable from the very presence of the other and from basic evaluations of goodness and badness. Even in the paranoid-schizoid position guilt appears in moments of integration (Klein, 1948) and is internal to all relations between integrated, separate persons.[33]

Klein's account of reconciliation advances Freud's also in that it applies to the girl's as neatly as it applies to the boy's post-Oedipal reconciliation. The Kleinian view of ethics and the Oedipus complex can promote our understanding of reconciled politics. According to Klein, the resolution of the Oedipus complex coincides with a successful working-through of the depressive position, namely, with the establishment of an integrated, predominantly benevolent, object-world. The depressive position and the Oedipus complex are both resolved in the establishment of a predominantly good and stable object-world in which *both private and public spheres* are represented and endorsed. This double resolution produces the reconciled position. Indeed, according to Klein, this general resolution results in mature object relations involving *reconciliation* with self, other and world. In Kleinian

---

[32] Though Klein disagrees with Freud's conception of the narcissistic origin of the ego ideal.

[33] "The synthesis between the loved and hated aspects of the complete object gives rise to feelings of mourning and guilt which imply vital advances in the infant's emotional and intellectual life." (Klein 1946, 178)

terms, the authoritarian personality's good self is weak and split off; it cannot be recognized and reconciled to the world. The good self of the alienated liberal is reconciled to the private sphere alone, while the reconciled liberal's good self is reconciled to both spheres. When Freud's and Klein's perspectives are combined, reconciliation emerges as the acceptance of one's inherited identity as a separate, autonomous, morally accountable individual, on the basis of the good-self's trust of self and others.[34]

[34] In the next chapter we shall see how this conception of reconciliation is anticipated in Nietzsche's moral psychology.

4. Alienated Liberalism

Alienated Liberalism

The last position in our introductory diagram is characterized by a combination of recognition in the private sphere and misrecognition in the civic sphere. Maternal recognition establishes the two spheres as firmly differentiated from each other. The alienated liberal inhabits both spheres: the intimacy of the one and the universality, separation and distance of the other. The differentiation between the two spheres is particularly evident for occupants of the alienated position. Each sphere is experienced in a distinct way. One is a sphere of domestic security, the other – of persecution and vulnerability. Depriving its alienated members of a sense of membership, the public sphere becomes the consummate contrast to the private sphere. According to Shoham, left wing ideologies strive to reverse the passage that takes place in the course of socialization from the secure private sphere – the household – into a hostile civic sphere. The alienated liberal refuses to give up the unconditional recognition received in the household, "the permissive irresponsibility of childhood participation" (Shoham 1978, 247).

> The goal of anarchy is the annihilation of the group structures so that the individual again reigns supreme... By destroying the groups that forced one out of the family fold in cruel rites of passage so that one switches allegiance to it, by annihilating the structures that coerced one into normative subordination and confined one in a prison cage of rules, one hopes to retain the blissful participation of childhood... What does the destroyer wish to achieve? To this we have a Camusian answer that the goal of the rebel is unity. (Shoham 1978, 200-1)

The alienated liberal's good self is firmly individuated only in the private sphere. Due to civic misrecognition, the alienated liberal cannot occupy the civic sphere as an integrated good self on the basis of mature identification with authority. Despite their alienation, alienated liberals may participate in the civic sphere actively. They inhabit all of social structure's differentiated spheres, occupy high positions and exercise their authority with a republican sense of duty without loosing anything of their alienation.

Civic misrecognition produces in the alienated liberal a bad 'civic self'. The civic sphere becomes a domain of persecution and self-hate.[1] Instead of mature identification based on mutual recognition between separate individuals, the alienated liberal's relation to the civic sphere is symbiotic and masochistic. In Kleinian terms, the alienated liberal, while in the civic sphere, remains in the schizoid-paranoid position under the influence of paranoid terror of totemic hegemony.[2] In terms of Alford's group psychology, the alienated liberal's schizoid-paranoid position *vis-à-vis* the political sphere is a "schizoid compromise": the alienated liberal defensively holds back his "best parts" since they are felt to be threatened by the group (Alford 1996, 116). In terms of the classical account of paranoia, the alienated liberal projects aggression onto the civic sphere, instigating political paranoia. This is Freud's account of paranoia – largely endorsed by Klein – which describes, at least in its general outlines, the alienated liberal's relation to the civic sphere. As Freud writes,

> People who harbor fantasies of [paternal punishment] develop a special sensitiveness and irritability towards anyone whom they can put among the class of fathers. They allow themselves to be easily offended by a person of this kind, and in that way (to their own sorrow and cost) bring about the realization of the imagined situation of being beaten by their father. I should not be surprised if it were one day possible to prove that the same fantasy is the basis of the delusional litigiousness of paranoia. (1919, 195)

The alienated liberal's maneuvers in the civic sphere are careful and

---

[1] The self-hate of the liberal intelligentsia is a hidden recurrent theme in G.L. Mosse's *Nationalism and Sexuality* (1985, 37, 73, 189).

[2] As Meltzer writes, political rebelliousness "characterized by... resentment of authority... is dominated by persecutory anxiety and prone to violent means and the expectation of violent retaliation..." (1973, 154).

guarded. While in the civic sphere, the alienated liberal relates to imaginary persecutors rather than separate, integrated individuals. As in the case of authoritarian paranoia, alienated paranoia is inseparable from sado-masochism.[3] Revenge and envy of forbidden paternal enjoyments may find expression in fantasies of 'magic annihilation' of civic authority. Alongside such sadistic fantasies, that, as we shall see in the next section, found various revolutionary outlets, there is a masochistic attitude to the hegemonic patriarchal totem. In "A Child is Being Beaten" Freud discusses alienated masochism and traces sado-masochism and paranoia to a disturbed relationship to the father/Father.

The beating fantasies Freud analyzes are only the first in a series of punishment fantasies entertained by the alienated liberal. If some people's attitudes to punishment reflect fear of crime (or, fear of their own badness, projected onto the criminal), other attitudes – including, notably, those of alienated liberals – reflect fear of authority. Kafka, who admitted that the terror of his father never left him (Kafka 1953, 17, 23), made the punishment fantasy his main literary theme. Joseph K. is convicted in advance of violating an arbitrary unknown law that applies only to him. Camus' *Stranger* is another variation on the same theme. Girard, in an essay on Camus (1988), describes the narrator of *The Stranger* as an instance of the familiar figure of the 'romantic personality.' Tracing the romantic personality's social ambivalence to its pride, Girard captures the essence of alienated liberalism:

> Why does Camus crave solitude and society at the same time; why is he both repelled and fascinated by *Les Autres*? The contradiction is really inherent in the Romantic personality. The Romantic does not want to be alone, but to be seen alone. In *Crime and Punishment*, Dostoyevski

---

[3] Following Freud's suggestions, Bak (1946) defined paranoia as delusional masochism. Freud relates paranoia and the beating fantasies to homosexuality: "In both cases the beating phantasy has its origin in an incestuous attachment to the father... The boy evades his homosexuality by repressing and remodelling his unconscious phantasy: and the remarkable thing about his later conscious phantasy is that it has for its contents a feminine attitude without a homosexual object choice. By the same process, on the other hand, the girl escapes from the demands of the erotic side of her life altogether. She turns herself in phantasy into a man, without herself becoming active in a masculine way, and is no longer anything but a spectator of the event which takes the place of a sexual act... it is precisely in unmanly boys and unwomanly girls that these beating-phantasies appeared and went through these vicissitudes..." (Freud 1919, 198-202)

> shows that solitary dreams and the 'Trial' are the two inseparable facets, the dialectically related moments of the Romantic consciousness. But this proud consciousness refuses to acknowledge openly the fascination it feels for the others. But the unacknowledged urge to return to other men is also stronger than ever. And this second urge can no longer be satisfied within the context created by the first. The murder is really a secret effort to establish contact with humanity. It reveals an ambivalence that is present in all art with solipsistic tendencies... (Girard 1988, 24)

This reclusive attitude Girard highlights – a paradoxical attitude of religious longing for social participation accompanied by social alienation – is anticipated in Fromm's and Klein's argument that symbiotic object relations are sado-masochistic. Through beating and punishment fantasies the alienated liberal seeks sado-masochistic symbiosis with the civic sphere. There are no enduring identifications and mature object relations that would secure an inbuilt non-paranoiac value-system of a strong good self and a stable group identity. Only within the private sphere do alienated liberals experience freedom, self-knowledge and integrity with their immediate environment. In the civic sphere, social misrecognition produces troubled ethical and group identity. There is no internalization of social values by a good self attached to a good civic sphere, nor that natural knowledge of good and bad considered by the common law a condition for criminal responsibility. Joseph K. never understands for which crime he is tortuously tried and executed.

Except for being too typical, some of the manifestations of Rousseau's paranoia and schizoid condition constitute textbook examples of the position of alienated liberalism. A banished citizen of Geneva, alienated from the civic sphere, Rousseau challenged paternal rights all his life and championed the maternal and the private. Rousseau's philosophy announced the end of the friction between individual and state and, incompatibly, the return to nature or to intimate and sheltered communities. Rousseau craved fame but could not bear applause when he won it, voluntarily clinging to poverty and humble position and making the exaltation of solitude one of the most characteristic leitmotifs of his oeuvre. Projecting all his bad parts onto others and being exceedingly envious, he avoided not only authority but hospitality and companionship as well. Companionship threatened him with attacks of envy and the return of projected aggression. The degree of Rousseau's paranoia[4] was

---

[4] Rousseau's *Rêveries de promeneur solitaire*, for example, abounds with

so high that nobody – no external object – was allowed to be good and win Jean Jacques' trust. Rousseau's noble savage is so pure and good because his bad parts are projected onto other people; he could not be really solitary. Rousseau is trapped in the paradoxes Girard attributes to the romantic personality, and it is well known that he was the favorite philosopher of the romantics.

Like Rousseau's *Confessions*, Kafka's confessional letter to his father and Girard's account of the romantic personality, Adorno describes a personality *defined* by its rejection of totemic authority.[5] At the end of his contribution to *The Authoritarian Personality*, Adorno distinguishes between five liberal personalities. The five accounts are somewhat arbitrary and not sufficiently worked out. One of them, the "protesting" liberal, has much in common with the alienated liberal. The protesting liberal is characterized by an uncompromising defiance of social authorities and a quest for an abstract, secular and anti-traditional authority. Adorno rightly observes that the alienated liberal defies civic authority *from within* the civic sphere.

> ...the further-going sublimation of the father idea, concomitant with an undercurrent of hostility against the father, leads to the conscientious rejection of heteronomous authority instead of its acceptance... While they are set against paternal authority, they have at the same time internalized the father image to a high degree. One may say that in them the super-ego is so strong that it turns against its own 'model', the father, and all external authorities. They are thoroughly guided by *conscience* which seems to be, in many cases exhibiting this pattern, a secularization of religious authority.[6] (Adorno *et al.* 1950, 771, 774)

Civic misrecognition can be established in a variety of ways, often through the mediation of one's father and prior to any explicit political

---

paranoid delusions.

[5] See the next section for Hegel's view of the pure negativity of alienated liberalism.

[6] Adorno continues insightfully as follows: "This conscience, however, is quite autonomous and independent of outside codes. They 'protest' out of purely moral reasons against social repression or at least against some of its extreme manifestations, such as racial prejudice. Most of the 'neurotic' low scorers who play such a large role in our sample show the 'Protest' syndrome. They are often shy, 'retiring', uncertain about themselves, and even given to tormenting themselves with all kinds of doubts and scruples."

involvement. When the Oedipus complex is not resolved into a mature, empowering and individuating identification with the father/Father, the entire hegemonic order may be repudiated. The young Kafka's fear of his father becomes a fear of the law. Sartre invokes a process of social estrangement based on the identification of father with society. "A man who suffers from a secret love of his mother feels guilty towards his father. He therefore has himself punished by society which is identified with the paternal authority..." (Sartre 1949, 90).[7] Through its subjection to unjust social sanctions, Sartre notes, the romantic personality reduces its own guilt: "For if good is less good, evil becomes less evil."

Civic misrecognition does not necessarily derive from actual paternal misrecognition. It can be mediated by *social misrecognition of the father* or by the *father's misrecognition of the civic sphere.* Social misrecognition is often constituted by social misrecognition of one's kinship unit. One's self-respect is mediated by the inter-group position of the sub-group to which one belongs. Recognition is, then, primarily a relation between totems, those of small as well as vast kinship units. The state and its institutions constitute the kinship framework of the nation as a whole, within which smaller kinship units are organized and classified as true members or as semi-strangers.[8] Nuclear families are often misrecognized, as a whole, when one of the parents is misrecognized due to belonging to a certain stigmatized minority. This explains better than interest-based explanations – with which it is compatible – support of the left among social minorities. Studies of voting patterns in the beginning of the century demonstrated that Jews in Europe and America consistently voted for socialist and liberal parties. If the 'Jewish mother' is more than a myth, alienated liberalism is only too predictable a result of misrecognition in the civic sphere accompanied by recognition – often considered excessive – in the private sphere.[9] Recognition is a mutual relation which can be avoided by the family as much as it can be avoided by society, for example, by a cynical, alienated reaction to the claims and demands of the civic sphere. Kafka portrays his father as abusive not only of his family members but of the external world outside the family.

As we saw in the context of the authoritarian personality,

---

[7] Translation revised. For the original see Sartre (1947, 106).

[8] See Fortes' (1969) elaborate discussion of the construction of societies as kinship groups and its implications.

[9] On Judaism and the left see Mendelsohn (1997).

misrecognition reproduces very easily. The reproduction of misrecognition does not give rise to much optimism. A cautiously pessimistic view of history has been present in psychoanalytic thought at least since Freud's *Civilization and its Discontents*, though it was occasionally contested by thinkers such as Fromm and Marcuse. Parents who suffered misrecognition in the private sphere tend to misrecognize their children, for example, by treating their children as narcissistic extensions in order to compensate for the misrecognition they themselves have suffered (Miller 1981, 67-71). Misrecognition in the social sphere also reproduces easily, since the social position of the child is mediated by the social position of its parents, and for the former reason (compensatory parental misrecognition) as well. Examples such as Kafka's father suggest that misrecognition in either sphere tends to spill over into the other sphere. The young Kafka finds himself persecuted in both spheres. Humiliation by his father within the family circle proved inseparable from his feeling that he lived in an unusually unhappy family, excluded from the happy world outside (Kafka 1953, 27).[10]

In terms of classical psychoanalytic theory, harsh examples of paternal misrecognition, such as the case of Kafka, illustrate exceptions to the 'normal' course of the Oedipus complex. This should not be taken to imply that girls cannot suffer from paternal misrecognition and find themselves in the alienated position. When the source of paternal misrecognition is the hegemonic Father, and even when it is the father, girls can be driven to the alienated position. It is possible that misrecognition by the mother, as well, can lead the daughter to the alienated position. When maternal misrecognition does not frustrate the girl's individuation-separation, it may still constitute civic misrecognition. To the extent that the mother serves as a civic role-model to her firmly individuated daughter, misrecognition on the part of the mother – as an agent of the hegemonic, patriarchal normative system[11] – may produce alienation from this normative system as a whole.

In the case of alienated liberalism, difficulties in the resolution of the Oedipus complex do not stem from pre-Oedipal maternal misrecognition and ego weakness (as they do in the case of authoritarianism), but from

---

[10] For another illuminating literary account of the psychology of alienated liberalism see Vargas-Llosa's novel *The Real Life of Alejandro Mayta* (1986).

[11] On the patriarchal scaffolding of the institutional systems of the West, see Legendre (1996).

the individual's failure to identify with the hegemonic totem. In terms of the jural aspect of identification, this is a failure to appropriate a social position, a social territory and the status of membership.[12] According to Freud, at the starting point of the Oedipus complex the child simultaneously admires and resents the parent of the same sex. A hostile father can produce a heightened castration anxiety, one which cannot diminish sufficiently to allow for a successful resolution of the complex. The father may be by and large *denied* to alleviate anxiety as the child restricts himself to the maternal world. As Kafka observes, the good comforting mother might interfere with individuation in relation to the father by offering a protective shelter and by sparing the child of confrontation with the aggressor. Freud (1938) described the defense mechanism of splitting in the face of castration anxiety as a simultaneous recognition of the paternal authority and denial of castration. When the father appears as thoroughly hostile and the child is firmly individuated the father figure *as a whole* may be estranged and split off, not only its threatening, castrating aspect. The Oedipus complex is sidestepped, a process Grunberger ascribes to the pathological narcissist who "shrinks from the Oedipus and identification because of the *visceral connotation of the process*, which he sees as penetration within his boundaries..."[13] (Grunberger 1979, 290). The object (the father) is seen as thoroughly bad and persecutory. Both Freudian and Kleinian theory would explain the formation of the alienated liberal's paranoia by invoking a process of projection. The father is made bad by the aggression projected onto him by the child.[14]

Alienated denial of the father does not diminish dependence on him as a source of social recognition and membership.[15] It implies a

---

[12] The concept of identification has legal dimension captured by the notion of 'universal succession' that denotes the transmission of the entire legal status of one person to another person.

[13] This accounts for some of the partial similarities between the alienated liberal and the authoritarian narcissist.

[14] In cases of 'normal' attachment to the father, there are also, at first, fusion and projective identification – expressed, for example, in regressive punishment fantasies – which are gradually replaced by mature, individuating identification.

[15] As the "principle of legitimacy" discovered and formulated by Malinowsky implies, social legitimacy universally depends on the recognition of both legally recognized parents.

renunciation of these goods. Even if a certain acceptance of castration always takes place, here political castration is accepted as a *fait accompli.*[16] The fear of the father neatly follows the path which Freud outlined in "A Child is Being Beaten" and interferes with the establishment of mature identification. The relation to the father becomes sado-masochistic, paranoid and dominated by Kafkaesque punishment fantasies.[17] For the alienated liberal, the paternal-civic object[18] is persecutory and unambiguously bad (unintegrated). An omnipotent, disparaging relation to the persecutory object is meant to strengthen the ego, partly by denying the ego's own aggression and drive for reparation.[19] Hate may be further fuelled by envy of phallic paternal enjoyments.

Less extreme than splitting the Father off is a perpetual fierce confrontation with authority, though such cases do not necessarily fall under the category of alienated liberalism. Meltzer describes this rebellious character:

> Rebelliousness embraces all those states related to the height of the Oedipus complex in which the struggle against the incest barrier is still in the forefront. It is characterized by contempt for the past, greed for power, resentment of authority, idealisation of novelty and disbelief in the importance of experience to the development of wisdom. It is dominated by persecutory anxiety and prone to violent means and the expectation of violent retaliation... Vendetta is the ethos and talion its rationale. (Meltzer 1973, 154)

---

[16] See Freud (1909) on acceptance of castration. The probable result is perpetual terror of the father/Father and possible identification with the mother. On the boy's identification with the mother see Freud (1922; 1923a, 34). According to Freud, the alienated liberal's identification with the mother may induce homosexual object choice. It can be speculated that acceptance of castration within a positive, ongoing attachment to the father may produce 'reconciled homosexuality'.

[17] On the body image that results from paternal misrecognition / castration see Gilman (1995).

[18] For Klein, it is primarily the father's penis.

[19] See Klein (1935, 134) on disparagement of the object. Klein writes: "This contempt, however, is also based to some extent on denial. He must deny his impulse to make extensive and detailed reparation because he has to deny the cause for the reparation, namely the injury to the object and his consequent sorrow and guilt." (Klein 1940, 152)

It has been sometimes argued that Oedipal failure can result also from a different process, in which castration anxiety is actually too weak. In such cases, Oedipal confrontation and challenge are avoided because the father is not sufficiently admired and feared. The father does not appear as a serious rival and does not represent the civic sphere, so that Oedipal tension dissolves. When the father is himself 'castrated', he is powerless to accord civic, totemic recognition. A probable result is that, in minority groups, for example, an apparent recognition on the part of one's particular father may fail to compensate for the social castration of that group.

The attitudes and ideals of the alienated liberal – ideals of the household paradigm and of universal self-realization – reflect his safe position in the private sphere and his alienation from the civic sphere. Excellence, as much as transgression, becomes a means of challenging and defying paternal authority, from whose domain and grace the alienated liberal is excluded. Recognition is often refused in dramatic gestures, though sometimes, when the sense of social misrecognition is tempered, the alienated liberal may keep pursuing his calling with a depressive, reconciled twist. The alienated liberal has good reason to choose spheres of excellence, such as, science and the arts, which conceal his intensely ambiguous attitude towards civic membership and do not make his alienation a disadvantage. Thanks to ample recognition in the maternal sphere, the alienated liberal's alienation does not prevent him from pursuing achievements that are recognized by hegemony.[20] Unlike the authoritarian personality, the alienated liberal is not anti-hegemonic in essence. He is opposed to assertions of totemic identity that come at the expense of universal principles, not to structural hegemony as such.

Spared many of the hardships of latency age, the alienated liberal may develop a true sense of justice earlier than the reconciled liberal. Paranoiac anxieties may be plentiful but these do not interfere with the sense of justice and, according to some detractors of justice, even foster it. The highest, post-conventional, stage in Kohlberg's developmental scheme seems to be the alienated liberal's starting point, because of the latter's general critical attitude towards society. Alienated politics heralds principles of universal recognition, human rights and universal welfare as substitutes for social recognition, of which the alienated liberal is deprived. The alienated liberal claims rights that protect individual from

---

[20] By contrast to other kinds of alienation, which are marked by indifference to achievement. On indifference to achievement, see Shoham (1979, 42).

society and seeks to imprint the household paradigm in the civic sphere. Marx's ideal of a communist society has been interpreted as a retreat to the maternal principle.[21] The alienated liberal's attitude to democracy is ambiguous. Like Rousseau, he does not trust the 'goodness of the common people' yet nor would he, in most cases, trust an anti-democratic elite, unless it is a liberal-socialist one.

In the following sections, the foregoing sketch of alienated liberalism will be supplemented by further observations taken from the theories which inspired it. An exposition of Hegel's criticism of the French Revolution and the Enlightenment will be followed by a discussion of Nietzsche's critique of liberalism.

Abstraction and Terror

Alienated liberalism, according to Hegel, negates existing *ethical life* and does not conceive of individuality and universality as concretely embodied in tradition. It starts from dissatisfaction with existing *ethical life*, an empty denial of tradition and social conventions grasped as arbitrary. Hegel (1942, 4) refers to the alienated liberal's total repudiation of *ethical life* as "godlessnes," that is, a complete negation of society's representations of its own unity.[22] For the reconciled liberal, as opposed to the alienated liberal, individuality and universality are embedded in concrete *ethical life* and confined to concrete historical limits. Hegel leveled many different criticisms against Enlightenment liberalism. These have to be carefully distinguished, like the different brands of Enlightenment liberalism itself. Hegel's criticism of liberalism consists of many arguments, each picking on a different moment of the Enlightenment and its ramifications. Hegel treats Kantian morality and utilitarianism separately and his critique of the French Revolution does

---

[21] See Fromm's papers on mother right in *The Crisis of Psychoanalysis* (1970) and work in anthropology on the thesis of matriarchal 'primitive communism'.

[22] Habermas wrongly attributes to Hegel an assertion of the "atheism of this [as opposed to the moral] world": "Insofar as in so doing philosophy criticizes the moral world as fragmented in itself, it thus asserts the 'atheism' of this world. But how can the high-handed judgement which Hegel pronounces in the preface to his *Philosophy of Right* on just this atheism of the moral world be reconciled with this? Obviously he has revised the position he has espoused in the earlier political writings." (Habermas 1974, 130)

not merely repeat his critique of the Enlightenment but develops it, to mention just some examples. Not all the flaws of Enlightenment liberalism Hegel invokes are essential components of alienated liberalism.

According to Hegel, the various ideals of the Enlightenment reflected the disintegration of historical *ethical life*, which was corrupted by aristocratic *culture*, and the consequent historical groundlessness of the civilized subject. As a result of groundlessness, reason withdraws from the world, concentrates into itself and enunciates "...baseless abstractions and positively stated negations such as freedom, equality, the pure state, etc…" (Hegel 1975a, 68). This withdrawal of reason into itself and its self-grounding in its own postulates is discussed in the *Phenomenology* as the "moral view of the world." The ideals of the Enlightenment are, in fact, forms of *faith* on a par with the religious faith that the Enlightenment denounced.[23] In this sense, the Enlightenment contradicts itself (Hegel 1977c, 365-74). In its various and contradictory instances, the flight to the world of faith derives from the breakdown of objective traditions and the ensuing groundlessness of the subject.

Reason's turn inwards precipitates an endless pursuit, baseless and hopeless, of inner self-realization, inner abstract virtue, perfection and purity.[24] Hegel's critiques of the emptiness and destructiveness of Kant's categorical imperative reformulate different aspects of these basic complaints (Ameriks 1987; Habermas 1990, 195-217). Like abstract Kantian individuals and duties, the abstractions of utilitarianism and civil

---

[23] Hegel discussed the relations between faith and reason already in his early essay *Faith and Knowledge* (1977b).

[24] Different ideals of reason and freedom reflect the positions from which they are projected. The conflicting Hegelian and Kantian conceptions of practical reason are rooted in different relational self-definitions. The Kantian reason-based conception of individual freedom is seen, from a Hegelian perspective, as rooted in social misrecognition. In Kant, reason is independent of tradition and authority providing a universal criterion of recognition. Agassi and Fried implicitly relate radical conceptions of reason with the paranoia characteristic of alienated liberalism: "Talented youths who discover the conventional nature of their institutions naturally tend to view convention as hypocritical and thus undeserving of any attention of a righteous man. This already leads them to the verge of paranoia, accentuated by the loneliness to which they thus throw themselves. When they mature they learn to live with convention, perhaps at the cost of a measure of self contempt." (Fried and Agassi 1976, 70)

society also reflect groundlessness. The Enlightenment rejects any form of historical grounding and justification of authority, and postulates instead abstract and empty standards of legitimacy, such as, utility, absolute freedom and the general will.

> ...when these abstract conclusions came into power, they afforded for the first time in human history the prodigious spectacle of the overthrow of the constitution of a great actual state and its complete reconstruction *ab initio* on the basis of pure thought alone, after the destruction of all existing and given material. The will of its re-founders was to give it what they alleged was a purely rational basis, but it was only abstractions that were being used; the Idea was lacking; and the experiment ended in the maximum of frightfulness and terror. (Hegel 1942, 258A)

Abstract reason tears itself apart from the historical world, from *ethical life*, and seeks to realize itself. The realization of abstract reason and absolute freedom can only signify the eradication of the concrete and arbitrary traditions and institutions of *ethical life*. Anything *given* is perceived as a constraint and provokes destructiveness.

> This undivided Substance of absolute freedom ascends the throne of the world without any power being able to resist it...What made the Notion into an existent *object* was its diremption into separate *subsistent* spheres, but when the object becomes a Notion, there is no longer anything in it with a continuing existence; negativity has permeated all its moments.... In this absolute freedom, therefore, all social groups or classes which are the spiritual spheres into which the whole is articulated are abolished; the individual consciousness that belonged to any such sphere, and willed and fulfilled itself in it, has put aside its limitation... (Hegel 1977c, 357)

When absolute freedom with its pure negativity seizes power, it is not capable of producing anything positive – as Nietzsche later stated in the same words – since production requires particular will.[25] Absolute freedom strives to destroy every instance of given, historical particularity. It eradicates traditional social structure and assumes the form of terror in turning against what remains: atomized individuals whose arbitrary particularity, that has become even more groundless, negates abstract reason (Hegel 1977c, 359-60). When absolute freedom and the general

---

[25] "Les girondins firent des vains efforts pour mettre en activité des lois quelconques après la mort du roi; mais ils ne purent faire accepter aucune organisation sociale: l'instinct de la férocité les repoussait toutes", writes Madame de Staël (1818, 287).

will objectify themselves in action, this action can only assume the form of murderous destruction.[26]

Hegel considered alienated liberalism as a historical condition for reconciled liberalism. The radical negation of the French Revolution constituted a necessary step on the way to the modern state. Radical negation ends in a return home and reconciliation. This is a dialectic many liberals experience individually, as did Hegel himself. Furthermore, Hegel never reproaches the Revolution for its violence but only for its a-historical philosophy. Terror was essential for the advent of the post-revolutionary world. In some ways, Hegel's dialectical appreciation of the French Revolution resembles other Nineteenth-century accounts. Hegel's analysis has affinities with Nietzsche's critique of liberalism and suggests itself as a possible outline of other bloody revolutions.

The psychological comments of Hegel's contemporaries on the Revolution – far too numerous to be discussed here – often contribute to the psychology of alienated liberalism in ways similar to Hegel's own contribution. Chateaubriand, for example, noted the totalitarian nature of revolutionary perfectionism and *étatisme*, and of the very endeavor to uproot the people from its old habits and sentiments (1978, 79-90). Guizot takes destructiveness to be inherent to the insatiable revolutionary search for an a-historical basis for legitimacy (Guizot 1985, 372).

Madame de Staël describes the cruelty that underlies appeals to the common interest and to standards of formal justice.

> ...les révolutionnaires n'etaient plus que les prêtres d'un dieu Moloch, appelé l'intérêt de tous, qui demandait le sacrifice du bonheur de chacun. En politique, persécuter ne mene à rien qu'à la nécessité de persécuter encore... L'arbitraire sans bornes était leur doctrine; il leur suffisait de donner pour prétexte à toutes les violences le nom propre de leur gouvernement, le *salut public*: funeste expression, qui renferme le sacrifice de la morale à ce qu'on est convenu d'appeler l'intérêt de l'État, c'est-à-dire aux passions de ceux qui gouvernent. ...ils appelaient justice une égale répartition de malheur. (1818, 243, 300, 323)

Tocqueville, a recognized master of political psychology, brought to light the vicissitudes of envy – authoritarian envy, indifferent to liberty, rather than liberal alienated envy – underlying progressive ideals. In Tocqueville's analysis of the Revolution, we find also the Hegelian theme

---

[26] "[S]ubjective virtue, whose sway is based on disposition only, bring.... the most fearful tyranny." (Hegel, 1944, 450)

of rupture with tradition in the name of a general ideal of humanity. "With this grand notion of humanity in general was mixed an unnatural contempt for the time in which one lived and the society to which one belonged." (1987, 153) The Revolution turned out to be so radical and violent because of the abruptness of the rupture with tradition, the sudden transfer of power and the dissolution of all constraints on the use of power (1987, 204, 208). The Revolution was all embracing, not only political. All traditional institutions, habits and notions, civil and religious, were overturned.

> In the French Revolution, however, both religious institutions and the whole system of government were thrown into the melting pot, with the result that men's minds were in a state of utter confusion; they knew neither what to hold on to, nor where to stop.[27]

The French Revolution differed from other political revolutions not only in denouncing an entire existing social order, but in advancing a new abstract concept of humanity, a new 'faith', thus resembling religious wars. Here, again, Tocqueville's analysis is similar to Hegel's:

> The French Revolution's approach to the problems of man's existence here on earth was exactly similar to that of the religious revolutions as regards his afterlife. It viewed the 'citizen' from an abstract angle, that is to say as an entity independent of any particular social order, just as religions view the individual, without regard to nationality or the age he lives in. It did not aim merely at defining the rights of the French citizen, but sought also to determine the rights and duties of men in general towards each other and as members of body politic. (1955, 12) [28]

Like Hegel, Tocqueville (1955, part II, chapter 11) demonstrates the

---

[27] *The old Regime and the French Revolution* (1955, 157). The entire social order had to be changed: "Since the object of the revolution was not merely to change an old form of government but to abolish the entire social structure of pre-revolutionary France, it was obliged to declare war simultaneously on all established powers, to destroy all recognized prerogatives, to make short work of all traditions, and to institute new ways of living. Thus one of its first acts was to rid men's minds of all those notions which had ensured their obedience to authority under the old regime. Hence its so markedly anarchic tendencies." (1955, 8)

[28] See also Tocqueville (1955, 13) on the attempt to ground legitimacy in universal a-historical laws. Madame de Staël, too, analyzes the Revolution in terms of religious fundamentalism (1818, 284).

sense in which liberty was more real under the constraints of the system of classes than in revolutionary democracy. Like Hegel, he illuminates revolutionary destructiveness, aversion to diversity and the despotism of revolutionary democracy:

> The form of tyranny sometimes described as 'democratic despotism'... was championed by the Economists well before the Revolution. They were for abolishing all hierarchies, all class distinctions, all differences of rank, and the nation was to be composed of individuals almost exactly alike and unconditionally equal. In this undiscriminated mass was to reside, theoretically, the sovereign power; yet it was to be carefully deprived of any means of controlling or even supervising the activities of its own government. For above it was a single authority, its mandatary, which was entitled to do anything and everything in its name without consulting it. (1955, 163) [29]

Hegel's account of the Revolution and those of his contemporaries make important contributions to the understanding of alienated liberalism. Hegel identifies the solipsistic inwardness, the empty negativity and the paranoiac manifestations (the ubiquitous suspicion underlying terror) of alienated liberalism and unearths the contradictions in which the alienated position is implicated. He captures the religious dimension of the alienated liberal's relation to the world, namely, liberal faith, which he calls "atheism" in accordance with his conception of religion as representation of the absolute unity of *ethical life*. Hegel intuits the fanatic nature of Enlightenment atheistic *faith* and the destructiveness, envy[30] and misrecognition underlying Enlightenment abstractions and formalism. It would be wrong, however, to generalize Hegel's account of the French Revolution, and to characterize alienated liberalism purely by the emptiness and negativity of its conceptions of universality, freedom and equality. Alienated liberals possess richly concrete private spheres which they strive to protect and enrich. Such

---

[29] See Tocqueville (1955, 164) on "subversive socialism" and (1955, 158) on the intolerance of diversity: "...they attacked not only specific forms of privilege but any kind of diversity whatsoever... and every obstacle to the achievement of this end should be done away with immediately."

[30] As Hegel writes of moral judgement, "...judgement is an expression of *envy* which covers itself with the cloak of morality" (1977c, 379). The workings of envy in morality and politics were later traced by Tocqueville and Nietzsche. See, for example, *Human, All Too Human* (Nietzsche 1994, 480).

aspirations make alienated politics partly positive and temper the misrecognition-based negativity that dominates authoritarian politics. It is the authoritarian personality, rather than the alienated liberal, that strives to destroy concrete forms of life (*ethical life*), thoroughly collapse separation and transcendence and turn structure into violent *communitas*. Alienated liberals aim to establish a strong structure with a liberal hegemony, in contrast to authoritarianism, which is hostile to hegemony and structure as such.

Political Ideals and the Will to Power, or: Action and Reaction in Liberalism

Nietzsche's distinction between slave and master morality relates attitudes to power and systems of ideals in ways that are recognizable in each of the three positions. The psychological mechanisms highlighted by Nietzsche can be integrated into the accounts of the three positions, even if it is impossible to regard any particular position as an instance of slave or master morality. In *The Gay Science* (1974, 118, 370), Nietzsche explicitly claims that certain ethical and political types can exemplify both master mechanisms and slave mechanisms. Nietzsche's characteristic ambiguity towards political ideologies would seem to entail, in the case of liberalism, praise for reconciled liberalism as an instance of master morality alongside derision of alienated liberalism as an existential strategy of the weak. However, even this generalization would be inaccurate, since Nietzsche does praise some aspects of alienated liberalism, such as heightened individuality and a certain striving for aloneness (1973, 26), while scorning some aspects of reconciled liberalism and of liberalism in general.[31]

---

[31] Such as values of freedom and democracy (as political freedom). The sensitivity to suffering that is reflected in liberal positions was one of Nietzsche's favorite objects of scorn (sections 2, 7 in *The Anti-Christ* (1968a). Like other aspects of slave morality, the sensitivity to suffering shows how modern socialism and democracy are transformations of Christianity and equally servile. Altruism is the instinct of self-preservation of the weak: "The preponderance of an altruistic mode of valuation is the consequence of an instinct that one is ill-constituted. The value judgement here is at bottom: 'I am not worth much'..." (Nietzsche 1968b, 373). On Nietzsche's critique of altruism see Kaufmann (1974, 338-411). The projects of optimistic social engineering, which set themselves to

The Nietzschean master's life assertion and *reconciliation* with the world do not necessarily involve actual displays of power. Walter Kaufmann argues convincingly that, according to Nietzsche, "great power reveals itself in great self mastery" (Kaufmann 1974, 251).[32] Moreover, self-mastery can reveal itself in justice. Nietzsche often speaks of justice positively. The essence of justice in a *community of masters* can be said to consist in reciprocity on the basis of self-love and mutual esteem (1994, 45, 92; 1967a, II 4, 11).[33] Nietzsche (1994, 216; 1967a, 72) notes that real social justice is a result of the self-overcoming of the master, and that only the master can be just.

This interpretation of master-morality as involving a certain vision of justice is shared by Mark Warren's brief reconstruction of Nietzschean political principles. Warren's reconstruction seems convincing, though the principles he articulates are not as distant from Nietzsche's text as he implies. Warren writes:

> If one wished to go further, to supplement Nietzsche's insights with a positive political vision, a vision consistent with his problematic, it would include the values of individuation, communal intersubjectivity, egalitarianism and pluralism... Individuation, in other words, is in many ways a collective achievement. The fabric of intersubjectivity that sustains individuals in turn implies the value of *equality* – not a levelling equality, but a vibrant equality based on an equal respect for persons and the condition of their personhood. Failure to value equality in this sense leads to exploitative relations that destroy the intersubjective reciprocity upon which a Nietzschean strength ultimately depends. (Warren 1988, 247)

---

fight poverty and crime, are life negating (Nietzsche 1968b, 40). The spread among the "strongest men" of the "religion of pity" and of the "mortal hatred for suffering in general... almost feminine incapacity to remain spectators of suffering, to *let* suffer..." is a mark of decline (Nietzsche 1973, 201-2).

[32] See the section "Of Self-Overcoming" in *Thus Spoke Zarathustra* (1969, 136-9). According to Kaufmann's introduction to *Ecce Homo* (1967b, 208), Nietzsche demonstrates in his account of himself how the master sublimates his "no-feeling." According to Warren (1988, 232), the will to power is a will for "self-constitution." This self-constitution involves a struggle of the individual against himself, by no means an essentially political conflict between individual and society.

[33] For a sympathetic view on social justice see *Human, All Too Human* (1994) sections 101, 451, 452, 457, 462.

The principles Warren purports to derive from Nietzsche's central conceptions of individuality and the will to power call to mind Hegel's political recommendations. To the extent that master morality cherishes the psychological value of mutual recognition and self-assertion, there would be much in common to a Hegelian and a Nietzschean psychological account of reconciled liberalism. Warren argues convincingly that Nietzsche's fundamental outlook is in many ways liberal and that his critique of liberalism resulted from false conceptions of modern society and economy which he entertained (Warren 1988, 237-47). Nietzsche's remarks on master morality can, at their best, illuminate the nature of reconciled liberalism as combining self-love, mutual respect, life assertion and a 'natural' way of handling power. However, to reiterate, reconciled liberalism cannot be plainly regarded as an instance of master morality due to Nietzsche's critique of values that would seem fundamental to the reconciled liberal.

Let us briefly consider in what ways liberalism can be considered as an instance of slave morality. Nietzsche's writings contain notorious denunciations of democracy, welfare-policies and leniency in sentencing.[34] Liberal positions are depicted as variants of slave morality or herd morality: democracy, socialism and anarchism, with their claims for liberty and equality, their "mistrust of punitive justice" and "religion of pity", represent a "counterattack" of the "suppressed race" (Nietzsche 1973, 202; 1967a, I 5). On several occasions Nietzsche refers to liberal principles as denials of life:

> ...everywhere one enthuses, even under scientific disguises, about coming states of society in which there will be 'no more exploitation' - that sounds to my ears like promising a life in which there will be no organic functions. 'Exploitation' does not pertain to a corrupt or imperfect or primitive society: it pertains to the *essence* of the living thing as a fundamental organic function, it is a consequence of the intrinsic will to power which is precisely the will of life. (Nietzsche 1973, 259)

The turn inward, conceived by Hegel as a denial of tradition, is seen by Nietzsche as a denial of life. As both Hegel and Nietzsche observed, the alienated withdrawal into inner realization generates dissatisfaction and

---

[34] Nietzsche detests bourgeois righteousness and indignation underlying punitive policies (1967a I 10, II 11, 14; 1968b 1(6), 124, 141, 196, 765, 1021) while ridiculing the lenient, reformist approaches to punishment (1973, 201; 1967a II 5-6, 9; 1968b, 739).

cruelty. According to Nietzsche, freedom and equality are turned into noble ideals by the weak, seeking peace and protection under their rule.

> 'Equality', a certain actual rendering similar of which the theory of 'equal rights' is only the expression, belongs essentially to decline: the chasm between man and man, class and class, the multiplicity of types, the will to be oneself, to stand out – that which I call *pathos of distance* – characterizes every strong age.[35]

This explanation of equality and freedom is eloquently presented in fragments that Nietzsche did not select for publication[36] and which were finally published in *The Will to Power*:

> One desires *freedom* so long as one does not possess power. Once one does possess it, one desires to overpower; if one cannot do that (if one is still too weak to do so), one desires 'justice', i.e., *equal power.* (Nietzsche 1968b, 784)

> Finally, the social hodgepodge, consequence of the Revolution, the establishment of equal rights, of the superstition of 'equal men'. The bearers of the instincts of decline (of *ressentiment*, discontent, the drive to destroy, anarchism, and nihilism), including the slave instincts, the instincts of cowardice, cunning and *canaille* in those orders that have long been kept down, mingle with the blood of all classes: two, three generations later the race is no longer recognizable – everything has become mob. From this there results a collective instinct against selection... (Nietzsche 1968b, 864)

Ideals of equality and liberty are not only denials of life and means of protection for the fearful. They are forms of an *inverted* will to power, weapons in the service of *revengeful resentment*. Through moral and political ideals, slaves "compensate themselves with imaginary revenge" (Nietzsche 1967a I 10):

> Whom amongst today's rabble do I hate the most? The Socialist rabble, the chandala apostles who undermine the worker's instinct, his pleasure, his feeling of contentment with his little state of being – who make him envious, who teach him revengefulness... Injustice never lies in unequal rights, it lies in the claim to *'equal'* rights... What is *bad*? But I have already answered that question: everything that proceeds from weakness, from envy, from *revengefulness*. The anarchist and the Christian have a

---

[35] "Expeditions of an untimely Man" par. 37 in *Twilight of the Idols* (1968a).

[36] See Magnus (1988).

> common origin... The Christian and the anarchist: both decadents, both incapable of producing anything but dissolution, poisoning, degeneration, both *bloodsuckers*, both with the instinct of *deadly hatred* towards everything that stands erect, that towers grandly up, that possesses duration, that promises life a future...[37]

Nietzsche captures the alienated liberal's destructive envy of forbidden master-enjoyments. According to Nietzsche, vengeful, "reactive" passions actually reveal self-hate. The Kleinian intuitions that revenge involves a degree of self-hate and masochism, and that sado-masochism and revenge are forms of self-preservation already underlie Nietzsche's fragments on slave morality. "The instinct of revenge and *ressentiment* appears here in both cases as a means of enduring, as the instinct of self-preservation: just as is the preference for altruistic theory and practice.... " (Nietzsche 1968b, 373)[38]

No less than the assertive ideals of master morality are the ideals of slave morality forms of will to power. In slave morality, the will to power manifests itself as a "reactive" force. It becomes an inverted will to power that transforms the slave's weakness into an ideal for the sake of self-preservation. In the following passage, Nietzsche's judgement of liberal 'individualism' is ambiguous. The passage is flanked by condemnations of individualism and is itself somewhat derogatory, yet the characterization of individualism as a "modest form of the will to power" is not entirely negative.

> *Individualism* is a modest and still unconscious form of the 'will to power'; here it seems sufficient to the individual to get free from an overpowering domination by society (whether that of the state or of the church). He does not oppose them as a person but only as an individual; he represents all individuals against the totality. That means: he instinctively posits himself as equal to all other individuals; what he gains in this struggle he gains for himself not as a person but as a representative of individuals against the totality... Socialism is merely a means of agitation employed by individualism... The preaching of altruistic morality in the service of individual egoism: one of the most common lies of the nineteenth century. Anarchism, too, is merely a means of agitation

---

[37] *The Anti-Christ* 57, 58 in *Twilight of the Idols* and *The Anti-Christ* (1968a). For more statements on revenge see "The problem of Socrates", fragment 7 and "Expeditions of an untimely man", fragment 34, in *Twilight of the Idols* (1968a).

[38] See also *The Gay Science* (1974) sections 370, 377 on anarchism as a destructive desire of the weak.

> employed by socialism; by means of it, socialism arouses fear, by means of fear it begins to fascinate and to terrorize... All this notwithstanding, individualism is the *most modest* stage of the will to power. (Nietzsche 1968b, 784)

In addition to Nietzsche's contribution to the understanding of reconciled liberalism, Nietzsche offers acute descriptions of some of the psychological motivations operative in alienated-liberal politics as a reversed form of the will to power. He notes the basic experience of dispossession and disempowerment which underlies various progressive political principles and ideals and the protective role of these ideals. His account of slave morality captures the results of misrecognition and disempowerment that were later highlighted by the Kleinian tradition, such as, revengefulness, envy of power and enjoyment, self-hate and sado-masochism. Like Hegel before him, Nietzsche captures the alienated turn inwards in the form of celebration of reason, the potential destructiveness of abstractions made in the name of reason and the masochistic redirection of aggression towards oneself in alienated liberalism. These and other parallels between the theoretical perspectives entertained in this book – whether Kleinian, Hegelian or Nietzschean – were only suggested in passing. Fuller exploration of these parallels and of the possibilities of restating and uniting the different perspectives remains to be done.

Appendix: Rationality and Discourse

Is a rational discussion – on the basis of *shared* convictions – of questions of justice that arise in the public sphere possible? Can occupants of different positions share moral assumptions and understandings of cultural objects, symbols and practices? Having discussed the various positions, let us briefly consider their implications on the nature of political discourse in the public sphere. It will be argued that, whatever may be the correct characterization of the different positions, rational debate between left and right over abstract questions of political justice is hardly possible.

Several models of ethical discourse and 'interpretation' have been propounded in recent years by moral philosophers such as Dworkin (1985), Taylor (1989), Rorty (1980), Walzer (1994), MacIntyre (1988) and Habermas (1990a). Some of these models were mainly motivated by the question of the possibility of rational dialogue in a pluralist public sphere. The influence of Kuhn's concept of paradigm is clearly visible in some models, such as Rorty's, MacIntyre's and Walzer's. In fact, Kuhn himself (1970, 92-93) applied the concept of paradigm to political discourse and proposed to understand breakdowns of political conversation as clashes of political paradigms. In science, crises come about when old paradigms are rendered dysfunctional. At some point, a new, revolutionary paradigm puts an end to the crisis. According to Kuhn, similar processes take place in politics. Political discontent generates alienation and struggle between political paradigms. This struggle is conducted outside established patterns of political action until a new pattern is institutionalized.

Habermas defends a more rationalist conception of public discourse. Since his first book, *The Structural Transformation of the Public Sphere*,

Habermas attempted to defend a certain conception of the public sphere which he takes to underpin democracy. Habermas developed an account of political discourse on the basis of his general theory of communicative action. His account of the nature of political *theory* assigns an important role to actual public discourse at the expense of philosophy's contribution. Participants in normative public discourse raise shared validity claims that inhere in the *life-world;* communicative action involves making claims in the name of a shared *reason.* "In these validity claims communication theory can locate a gentle, but obstinate, a never silent although seldom redeemed claim to reason, a claim that must be recognized de facto whenever there is to be consensual action." (Habermas 1979, 97) Communicative action consists in understanding these validity claims; they are "transcendental-pragmatic" in the sense that without prior grasp of them participation in discourse is impossible. Any attempt to deny these validity claims implicates the participant in a "performative contradiction," that is, in denial of the very presuppositions that he himself constantly draws on.

Communicative action *aims* at reaching a consensus and is *already* grounded in a consensus that resides in the life-world, where the shared validity claims are rooted.[1] Every sphere of discourse has its own validity claims. Habermas distinguishes between discourse on questions of justice and morality, where the validity claim implicit in each utterance is conformity with the principle of universalization, and discourse on questions of the good life, which is aimed at the articulation of an authentic form of life. Each realm of discourse rests on a shared, implicit historical knowledge of formal and substantial principles, which renders discourse rational.

Rawls has been concerned over the two last decades with a similar problem of securing a shared basis for discourse on questions of justice in a pluralist society. Rawls assumes that the only shared basis for public discourse can be found in a "political conception of justice", namely, a conception that is not derived from a comprehensive ethical and metaphysical doctrine (1993, 11, 154). Any comprehensive doctrine

---

[1] Entire social theories are often modeled on a fundamental account of action, and Habermas's concept of communicative action is indeed rich in theoretical implications. It encapsulates a *dialogical* account of human interaction ("a *telos* of mutual understanding is built into linguistic communication"; 1992a, 100) and a dialogical account of truth and validity claims as grounded in the consensus of the life-world.

would be contested in a pluralist society and fail to provide uncontested starting points for a rational discourse.

Rawls' conception of the scope of public reason is narrower than Habermas'.[2] Rawls excludes ethical, as opposed to moral, questions, and *truth* in general, as opposed to *reasonableness*, from the scope of public reason. The very distinction between ethical questions and questions of justice is elusive and questionable; it conceals a multitude of distinctions that draw different lines between the ethical and the moral in light of different rationales. In Habermas, the distinction between the ethical and the moral is drawn on the *philosophical* level where different "validity claims" are analyzed and distinguished. For Rawls, the distinction between the ethical and the moral has two levels, both intended to respond to moral-practical purposes. The Rawlsian bracketing of the ethical, as elaborated in *A Theory of Justice,* is a substantial moral requirement: a requirement of fairness to endorse the neutral point of view of the original position where basic constitutional principles are selected behind a veil of ignorance which neutralizes economic interests and ideological preferences. It is a requirement to treat every citizen in accordance with the general principles that he would have chosen for his own good in the original position. Fairness requires that the state impose duties on its citizens only in the name of a constitutional structure that each citizen would have opted for himself in the original position and that social cooperation be advantageous to all citizens. Rawls' second book, *Political Liberalism,* adds a further level of neutrality consisting in the neutralization of the ideal of fairness itself. Fairness is detached from its possible grounding in a liberal comprehensive doctrine, in order to facilitate the emergence of an "overlapping consensus" on fairness among citizens who subscribe to different comprehensive doctrines.

Before criticizing Rawls' and Habermas' rationalistic accounts of the public sphere – admittedly rationalistic in humble, 'postmetaphysical' ways – it has to be noted that both those who deny and those who acknowledge the possibility of rational disagreement on questions of political justice, seem to do so from a narrow conception of the ontology of political agreement and disagreement. While Kuhn may be correct in drawing the limits of political dialogue, his account of breakdowns in political discourse seems much less sound, and subsequent models inherit the weaknesses of his model. Whether or not science is political, politics is not scientific. Political conversation among occupants of different

---

[2] *See* Habermas (1995).

positions cannot be reduced to an encounter of different Kuhnian paradigms. Rorty and MacIntyre, for example, are mistaken in explaining the impossibility of dialogue in terms of incommensurable conventions, or conceptual schemes. Rorty's distinction between normal and abnormal discourse is plainly Kuhnian.[3] Kuhn's and Rorty's emphasis on conceptual paradigms unduly abstracts and privileges one single aspect of historical modes of being.

Habermas, too, is generally indifferent to the psychoanalytic and existential foundations of moral judgements.[4] Habermas prefers to ground moral judgements in cognitive categories of the life-world (without denying the psychological conditions that facilitate these judgements). Throughout his theory, Habermas describes socio-historical, political and cultural processes in terms of the vicissitudes validity claims undergo. For example, his account of the distortion of communicative action through the intervention of 'systems' primarily invokes the repression of the validity claims embodied in communicative action. His account of discourse focuses on the "argumentative redemption of validity claims" at the expense of hermeneutic-dialogical phenomena emphasized in the dialogical philosophies of Buber, Gadamer and others. While Gadamer's conception of everyday hermeneutics marks the broad boundaries within which Habermas' thought develops (notwithstanding Habermas' consideration of 'systems'), Habermas drifts to the opposite extreme, privileging a supposedly cognitive dimension of communicative action in his attempt to redress the balance "distorted" by Gadamer.

There are three kinds of agreement in Habermas' account of discourse. First, there is a general background agreement that resides in the inarticulate life-world. Second, there is a hypothetical dynamic agreement over the contents of the validity claims that are raised in each sphere of discourse and are articulated by philosophers. Finally, there is an anticipated consensus towards which discourse is oriented. Habermas

---

[3] "Normal discourse is that which is conducted within an agreed-upon set of conventions as to what counts as a relevant contribution, what counts as answering a question, what counts as having a good argument for that answer or a good criticism of it. Abnormal discourse is what happens when someone joins in the discourse who is ignorant of those conventions or who sets them aside." (Rorty 1980, 320)

[4] See, for example, his critiques of Tugendhat and Apel (Habermas 1993, 47, 80-84).

may be right in insisting that the production of consensus is an aim built into every discourse, including political discourse, even though it is seldom realized. However, the shared resources of the life-world are not rich enough to make rational debate over questions of political justice possible. As Rorty suggested, the validity claims Habermas articulates are either too formal and too general to stand for real agreement that could yield concrete decisions, or too controversial. Habermas' proceduralism seems to fail in overcoming the rifts between the different positions. Habermas recognizes the intractably dynamic hermeneutic flow of everyday discourse envisaged by Gadamer, yet perceives this discourse as structured by shared validity claims. In reality, discourse does not abide by such shared presuppositions.

Hebermas' idea that a participant who does not conform to the validity claims of the discourse commits a performative contradiction cannot be put to critical use. What counts as a contradiction cannot always be determined from a position outside the speaker's particular constellation of ideals, purposes and paradigms of social relations.[5] Different sets of evaluations – different psycho-political positions – endow an apparently shared principle with different senses and practical implications. Most often, there is not even an *apparent* agreement among occupants of different positions over a principle that could guarantee rationality as a meta-discursive principle.

It is the proceduralism propounded in Rawls' *Political Liberalism* that makes a more concrete and practical attempt to overcome *actual* political divisions. Rawls proposes to ground discourse in a shared "*political* conception of justice." He expects citizens in pluralist societies to share a neutral "political conception of justice" based on the general idea of fairness that is encapsulated in the model of the "original position." Rawls expects citizens to suspend their ethical convictions while acting in the public sphere, in order to create a pluralistic democracy which is a "well ordered society"[6] with a flourishing "public reason."

---

[5] Winch makes a similar point in his criticism of Evans-Pritchard's tendency to identify *contradictions* in the beliefs of the Zande. "...the context from which the suggestion about the contradiction is made, the context of our scientific culture, is not on the same level as the context in which the beliefs about witchcraft operate. Zande notions of witchcraft do not constitute a theoretical system in terms of which Azande try to gain a quasi-scientific understanding of the world." (Winch 1970, 93)

[6] "To say that society is well-ordered conveys three things: first (and implied by

Somewhat unfairly and paradoxically, Rawls' theory of justice is subject to sociological skepticism precisely due to its attempt to be down-to-earth, to take into account actual political processes and sketch a blueprint of its own implementation. Rawls' project of establishing an overlapping consensus is, in many ways, highly realistic. Rawls acknowledges the fact that *there is no rational dialogue between supporters of different comprehensive doctrines*, and argues that normative dialogue between them is only possible when it concerns 'procedural' fairness. Furthermore, Rawls admits that even this procedural dialogue is possible only in societies which already have a tradition of constitutional democracy and where pluralism is mild and "reasonable" rather than pervasive and extreme. Rawls also admits that even once an overlapping consensus is reached, disagreement remains pervasive: according to Rawls, in many cases the overlapping consensus functions only as a *shared mode of presentation*, a shared terminology used for the expression of incompatible claims made on behalf of different comprehensive doctrines. The overlapping consensus is a meta-language in which radically different claims may be cloaked and put forward in the public sphere.

Rawls' suggestion that "reasonable" people who subscribe to different comprehensive doctrines do share an elementary sense of procedural fairness, which could serve as a basis for an overlapping consensus, is illuminating. People who hold different comprehensive doctrines share notions of procedural fairness, and in many routine, 'easy' cases would agree about the demands of fairness. It is arguable that an elementary, universal sense of fairness conditions the possibility of cooperation in any group, irrespectively of its comprehensive doctrines. However, contrary to Rawls' hope, the shared sense of procedural fairness cannot produce agreement on general and fundamental questions of justice. As a *political conception of justice* – a theory of the "basic

---

the idea of a publicly recognized conception of justice), it is a society in which everyone accepts, and knows that everyone else accepts, the very same principles of justice; and second (implied by the idea of the effective regulation of such a conception), its basic structure – that is, its main political and social institutions and how they fit together as one system of cooperation – is publicly known, or with good faith believed, to satisfy these principles. And third, its citizens have a normally effective sense of justice and so they generally comply with society's basic institutions, which they regard as just. In such a society the publicly recognized conception of justice establishes a shared point of view from which citizens' claims on society can be adjudicated." (Rawls 1993, 35)

structure" of society – fairness becomes controversial.

Rawls' interpretation of fairness in terms of the original position and the two principles of justice will not enjoy the support of an overlapping consensus. As a *political* principle, fairness requires universal welfare, an ideal rejected by many who do accept notions of fairness while participating in smaller-scale frameworks of cooperation. The two underlying ideals of Rawls' project – the ideal of a "well ordered society" with an overlapping consensus as the basis for free and reflective citizenship, and the ideal of society as a "fair system of cooperation" with fairness interpreted in terms of the original position – would not be shared by occupants of the different positions. Put together, Rawls' two ideals articulate an image of society as a framework of free, fair and reflective cooperation. This noble image would not even be endorsed by many liberals. Traditionally, liberalism did not regard normative consensus in the public sphere as a condition for the freedom and self-realization of the individual. Nor did it view society as a fair system of cooperation but as the interaction matrix of egoistic agents making use of one another. Any attempt to derive a shared "political conception of justice" from elementary notions of fairness and from the political culture of constitutional democracy is doomed to fail in the face of fundamental political polarities. Rawls' project assumes the substantial ideals of "fairness" and "well-ordered society", which are not universally accepted even in societies with a tradition of constitutional democracy for which Rawls designs his theory. These ideals are characteristic of occupants of the reconciled position, as is the transition from a "constitutional" to an "overlapping" consensus or, to use Kohlberg's terms, from a conventional to a post-conventional political morality. Kohlberg's developmental model and the values it champions apply to occupants of the reconciled position. The same is true of Rawls' moral and developmental conceptions.[7]

Compared with Rawls' "overlapping" consensus, a "constitutional" consensus, namely, a consensus over the supreme authority of a certain sacred document, seems more feasible. It is a consensus over collective historical identity, like Durkheim's "collective consciousness," rather than a reflective and critical consensus over general principles of justice. Agreement on fundamental principles cannot be achieved, and the use of

---

[7] Rawls exercised a major influence on Kohlberg's account of the "post-conventional" stage. Later on, Rawls seems to have borrowed developmental concepts from Kohlberg.

the overlapping consensus as merely a mode of presentation, rather than a shared substantial ideal, cannot make disagreement rational. Rawls seems incorrect also in his assumptions concerning the relationship between reason, violence and civility in politics. According to Rawls, the absence of an overlapping consensus or, the impossibility of conducting a rational debate over questions of justice, pose a threat to political stability. However, differences in doctrine threaten political stability only when additional conditions trigger tensions. It is naive to suppose, as do Rawls and many other writers on pluralist and multicultural societies, that the problem of pluralist societies stems from disagreement over "comprehensive doctrines." While disagreement is often viewed as the source of a dangerous conflict, the real sources of violence usually lie elsewhere. Rival ideals can coexist peacefully. Chronologically, neither the emergence nor the waning of social conflicts coincide with the beginning or end of disagreement.[8]

---

[8] Rawls believes that a common public perspective has to be constructed and made historically efficacious. Fairness and stability will be collectively pursued from the rational collective point of view of the overlapping consensus. The possibility of such a rational historical agency seems doubtful. If violence can be banished from history – a hope Hegel did not share – the available means for achieving this are the civility and reasonableness of a "constitutional consensus," not an "overlapping consensus." It is arguable, however, that the relations between civility and reason are even more somber: violence may be seen as a condition for political civility. Many foundation myths preserve the memory of untold violence. The constitutional mythology and culture in America may be traced to the impact of the civil war, and contemporary social-democratic civility in Europe may be nothing more than a post-war compromise. Violence is arguably the only way out of certain conflicts, divisions and impasses. It may be a necessary condition for starting new social practices from scratch, for loosening the hold of old mythologies and conflicting totemic identities and for replacing them with new, more useful ones. When the dying Kojeve was told of the May 68 riots, he asked whether any blood was shed. To the negative answer he replied: "...then nothing has happened". According to Hegel, Spirit operates behind the backs of individual agents and occasionally resorts to violence on its way to self-knowledge. "[T]hat the spirit spends many races and generations of men at this labour of its self-knowledge, that it lays out a prodigious expenditure of coming-to-be and passing away, matters nothing to it. It is rich enough for expenditure on that scale; it paints with a large brush; it has nations and individuals enough to spend. There is a trivial saying that nature goes to its end by the shortest route – correct! But the route of the spirit is roundabout, mediation. Time, toil, expense – categories like these, drawn from finite life, are

While the assumption that disagreement is rational – that is, based on shared convictions – is misleading, it seems to be useful. Discourse itself does not stop when it becomes devoid of rationality. The very persistence of discourse makes possible the achievement of compromise when ideals remain radically different. According to the republican tradition, participation in the public sphere amounts to the highest form of human self-realization and this may be the case even if discourse is irrational. Geertz highlights a further creative function of irrational public discourse: collective sense seeking. Geertz advocates this new understanding of legal discourse: "a shift toward hermeneutic thinking about it – as a mode of giving particular sense to particular things in particular places (things that happen, things that fail to, things that might)" (1993, 232). On hermeneutic grounds Geertz argues for "the rejection of a consensus account of the practical force of law in favor of a sense-seeking one...., the argument that self-understanding and other understanding are as internally connected in law as they are in other realms of culture..." Various roles which Habermas attributes to communicative action can be equally performed by a non-rational discourse:

> Under the functional aspect of mutual understanding, communicative action serves to transmit and renew cultural knowledge; under the aspect of coordinating action, it serves social integration and the establishment of solidarity; finally, under the aspect of socialization, communicative action serves the formation of personal identities. (Habermas 1987, 137)

Furthermore, the assumption of a rational public sphere is partly constitutive of liberal and democratic practices.[9] However, the fiction of

---

irrelevant here." (Hegel 1985, 43-44) "A mighty figure must trample many an innocent flower underfoot, and destroy much that lies in its path." (Hegel 1975c, 89)

[9] Charles Taylor emphasizes that the operation of arenas of social action such as the public sphere assumes a certain shared self-understanding among the participants (Taylor 1995, 260-71). Taylor defines the public sphere too generally: "I want to describe it as a common space in which the members of society meet, through a variety of media (print, electronic) and also in face-to-face encounters, to discuss matters of common interest; and thus to be able to form a common mind about those matters" (1995, 259). While this definition omits the uniquely political dimension of the public sphere, Taylor nicely illustrates what is a common space: "It's a rather strange thing, when you come to think about it... two people [who] have never met... are seen as linked in a common space of discussion through media..." (1995, 261).

rational discourse may sometimes be damaging as liberals take it too seriously and refrain from using rhetorical means – of which the right wing amply avails itself – even when these means can be rhetorically reconciled with the fiction of rational discourse. The right-wing is much less discriminating in its choice of means, making its road to victory quicker and easier.

A recent discussion of the problem of the rationality of political disagreement is Andrew Mason's *Explaining Political Disagreement* (1993). Mason is right to choose the construction of a bridge between cognitivism and emotivism as his general aim and to call for an integration of rational and non-rational explanations of disagreement (1993, 15, 60). Moreover, there is sense in rejecting the interpretation of the cognitive element, the possession of truth-value, in terms of actual or potential convergence in moral reasoning. As Mason claims:

> ... if a concept is essentially contested, then it admits of a variety of different interpretations, more than one of which is reasonable. If a range of different interpretations is reasonable, this does not imply that none of them is best, nor that none can be justifiably regarded as best. But it does follow that when the strongest reasons favour one conception..., and hence that it can be justifiably regarded as the best, people who refuse to accept this conception in the face of these reasons (on the grounds that they are unpersuaded by them) need not be unreasonable even though they are mistaken. (1993, 53)

However, Mason offers no account or criterion whatsoever of what is cognitively reasonable or cognitively best. He offers no common standard to adjudicate between left and right. Mason fails to give a positive account because he rejects traditional concepts such as emotivism and cognitivism on the one hand, yet on the other hand, continues to formulate the problem in terms of the truthfulness of statements. Truth and reasoning in ethics are embodied in complex modes of being where reason and desire are inseparable.[10] The sort of

---

[10] According to Aristotle, the morally well-educated person finds pleasure in virtuous actions. The action of the virtuous man originates in a choice in which desire and deliberation coincide. *Nichomachean Ethics*, (1980, 28-35, 53-58). See also Broadie's discussion: "In rational choice, thought converges with desire..." (1991, 220). Hegel's analyses of historical modes of being consistently link categories of thought and existential welfare and he often criticized the Kantian divorce between concepts and concrete *ethical life*. "Yet self-conscious feeling, i.e. a thought, cannot discard feeling: there is no opposition between

agreement needed to sustain rational discussion over questions of justice that arise in the public sphere is agreement in intersubjective positions as modes of being. To conduct a rational agreement-based discourse, participants need to share not only a language, but also fundamental attitudes and existential concerns.

Occupants of the same position can not only agree rationally, but also disagree rationally. Participants in discourse do not have a privileged epistemic access to the degree of the rationality of their discourse, namely, to whether they share the same position. Each participant enters discourse with his own particular horizon. Even when participants share the same position, their basic shared values are differently represented, concretized and objectified within each participant's horizon. Conceptions of the Good are composed of fundamental ideals and concrete forms of everyday-life which, on account of our personal histories, we take to be good and to embody our fundamental ideals. The relations between ideals and the forms of life which objectify them are, to a large extent, historically contingent. In discussions over questions of justice, participants disagree rationally when they share the same basic values – the same position – without entirely sharing the forms of life that objectify these values yet approach a "fusion of horizons." Horizons fuse when participants gain sight of whatever separates their interpretations of the same basic ideals or, when the different interpretations become one in the course of discourse. Normative concepts are embedded in quotidian social practices where they are used with varying degrees of reflectivity. These concepts are first made available to us in the form of conventional paradigms that govern their usage in quotidian social practice. In normative discussions these concepts are, to a certain extent, liberated from their original, conventional settings. In this way, occupants of the same position can overcome differences between local-conventional paradigms and realize that they share the same basic values, the same position.[11]

Whatever the correct theory of political psychology may be, rational debate between left and right over abstract questions of political justice is impossible. While it is normally the case in political discourse that most participants use the same language of justice with good intent, many are not concerned with justice at all. In talking about justice, left and right are

---

feeling and thinking..." (Hegel 1985, 147)

[11] Dworkin's account of *essentially contested concepts* only succeeds in describing debates between occupants of the same position.

either motivated by radically different existential concerns or not equally motivated at all. Normative concepts used by the right are often borrowed from liberal and left wing traditions and then distorted and drained of meaning. Even the abstract purpose of articulating political principles (Dworkin's "interpretive attitude") is not shared by left and right. The scope of possible rational debate further decreases due to the fact that different historical sub-groups fight for hegemony: in extreme cases, there is not even a 'constitutional consensus', namely, a consensus regarding the authority of certain political scriptures. Such conflicts between sub-groups only multiply and complicate the irrational conflicts that separate occupants of the different positions. *Within* every sub-group divisions emerge between occupants of the different positions.

In certain cases, rational exchange between left and right over values that are effectively institutionalized, such as various procedural principles, is possible. More generally, there are rational exchanges concerning values shared by the bulk of the community. Such shared ideals typically include attachments to traditional features of society's form of life, shared models, values thought to regulate the everyday interaction of self and others (honesty, recognition, reciprocity, and so on) and ideals which exalt collective interests and the means for their protection. *Shared* idealizations of the existing political institutions – idealizations which make such institutions possible – provide common points of reference permitting the continuation of discourse. Other possible rational dialogues concern relatively *concrete* practical issues. The parliament and the press do not discuss, as a matter of course, abstract principles of justice. Concrete problems enable participants to formulate relevant concerns in concrete terms that can serve as a basis for collective action.

None of the categories of shared evaluations guarantees agreement on principles of justice. Shared evaluations may make some dialogue possible, but this does not extend to general questions of justice.[12]

---

[12] It may be argued that the rationality of discourse lies precisely in its ability to bypass fundamental disagreement and keep itself going. Theoretical arguments usually fail to rest on shared assumptions and change opinions, but this failure does not refute the rationality of normative discourse. According to this line of thought, discourse has to be perceived from a pragmatist perspective. As long as discourse manages to uphold frameworks of social cooperation, it is rational. The argument so far was indeed leveled against an argumentative, non-pragmatist paradigm of rational discourse. Narrow as this purely argumentative paradigm

Moreover, it is never possible to determine in advance whether or not a debate will be rational. Conflicting underlying concerns may emerge in the course of discourse, even when discourse initially revolved around a shared value or a concrete issue. In reality, there is typically a constant and rapid alternation between levels on which rational debate is possible and levels where the gap between outlooks is insurmountable. The preceding speculations need to be closely examined in light of empirical studies of the actual pragmatics of political discourse. Such studies will do more justice, in a deconstructive vein, to the dynamics of random formations of new contexts.

---

may be, it is implicitly assumed by most of the knights of rational discourse. While a detailed consideration of the pragmatist view of discourse exceeds the scope of the present discussion, it must be said that, at any rate, *pragmatism does not claim that anything that goes is rational*. It only suggests that reason, as well as unreason, are inseparable from modes of behavior and have an operational dimension.

Literature Cited

Abraham, K. 1920. Manifestations of the Female Castration Complex. In *Selected Papers on Psychoanalysis,* 338-369. London: The Hogarth Press and The Institute of Psychoanalysis

Adorno, T.W. 1946. Anti-Semitism and Fascist Propaganda. In *Anti-Semitism: A social disease*, ed. E. Simmel, 125-137. New York: International University Press.

———. 1967. Sociology and Psychology – I. *New Left Review* 46:67-81.

———. 1968. Sociology and Psychology – II. *New Left Review* 47: 79-97.

———. 1974. *Minima Moralia: Reflections from Damaged Life.* London: Verso

———. 1978. Freudian Theory and the Pattern of Fascist Propaganda. In *The Essential Frankfurt School Reader*, ed. A. Arato and E. Gebhart, 118-137 .Oxford: Basil Blackwell.

———. 1994. *The Stars Down to Earth.* London: Routledge.

Adorno, T. W., E. Frenkel-Brunswik, D.J. Levinson, and N. R. Sanford. 1950. *The Authoritarian Personality.* New York: Harper and Row.

Adorno, T. and M. Horkheimer. 1986. *The Dialectic of Enlightenment.* London: Verso.

Alford, C.F. 1996. *Group Psychology and Political Theory.* New Haven: Yale University Press.

Ameriks, K. 1987. The Hegelian critique of Kantian morality. In *New Essays on Kant*, ed. M. Moen and B. den-Ouden. New York: Peter Lang.

Anzieu, D. 1984. *The Group and the Unconscious*. London: Routledge.

Apostolides, J. M. 1981. *Le Roi-Machine, spectacle et politique au temps de Louis XIV*. Paris: Minuit.

Aries, P. 1981. *The Hour of our Death.* Trans. H. Weaver. New York: Knopf.

Aristotle, 1980. *Nicomachean Ethics.* Trans. D. Ross. Oxford: Oxford University Press.

———. 1995. *Politics*. Trans. Baker and Stalley. Oxford: Oxford University Press.

Assmann, A. 1994. *Construction de la Memoire. Une breve histoire de l'idee allemande de la Bildung*. Paris: Maison des Sciences de l'Homme.

Avineri, S. 1972. *Hegel's Theory of the Modern State*. Cambridge: Cambridge University Press.

Bachofen, J.J. 1973. *Myth, Religion and Mother Right*. Princeton: Princeton University Press.

Bak, R. C. 1946. Masochism in Paranoia. *The Psychoanalytic Quarterly* 15: 285-301.

Balandier, G. 1992. *Le pouvoir sur scènes*. Paris: Balland.

Barshack, L. 2000. The Subject of Ideals. *Cultural Values* 4 (1): 77-100.

Bataille, G. 1997. The psychological structure of fascism. In *The Bataille Reader*, ed. F. Botting and S. Wilson, 122-147. Oxford: Blackwell.

Benjamin, J. 1977a. The end of internalization: Adorno's Social Psychology. *Telos* 32: 42-64.

———. 1977b. Authority and the Family Revisited or, a World Without Fathers? *New German Critique* 13: 35-57.

Berke, J. E., S. Pierides, A. Sabbadini, and S. Schneider, eds. 1998. *Even Paranoids have Enemies.* London: Routledge.

Berliner, B. 1958. The role of object relations in moral masochism. *The Psychoanalytic Quarterly* 27: 38-56.

Bion, W.R. 1961. *Experiences in Groups.* London: Routledge.

———. 1967. The differentiation of psychotic from non psychotic patients, A theory of thinking. In *Second Thoughts.* London: Heinemann.

Borges, J.L. 1970. Deutsches Requiem. In *Labyrinths* Donald, ed. A. Yates and J. E. Irby, 173-180. Harmondsworth: Penguin.

Broadie, S. 1991. *Ethics with Aristotle.* New York: Oxford University Press.

Brooker, P. 1991. *Fraternalism: Nazi Germany, Fascist Italy, Imperial Japan.* Oxford: Oxford University Press.

Brunner, J. 1994. Looking into the Hearts of the Workers, or: How Erich Fromm Turned Critical Theory into Empirical Research. *Political Psychology* 15 (4): 631-654.

Bryson, N. 1990. Still Life and 'Feminine Space'. In *Looking at the Overlooked, four essays on still life painting,* 136-178. London: Reaktion books.

Burkert, W. 1983. *Homo Necans.* Berkeley: University of California Press.

Cervantes, M. 1950. *The Adventures of Don Quixote*. Trans: J.M. Cohen. Harmondsworth: Penguin.

Chasseguet - Smirgel, J. 1981. Feminine Guilt and the Oedipus Complex.

In *Female Sexuality*, 94-134. London: Maresfield.
———. 1985. *The Ego Ideal.* Trans. P. Barrows. New York: Norton.
Chateaubriand. 1978. *Essai sur les revolutions, Genie du Christianisme.* Paris: La Pleiade.
Chodorow, N. 1978. *The Reproduction of Mothering: Psychoanalysis and the Sociology of Gender*. Berkeley and Los-Angeles: University of California Press.
Davidson, D. 1982. *Inquiries into Truth and Interpretation.* Oxford: Oxford University Press.
Deleuze, G. 1991. Coldness and Cruelty. In *Masochism.* New York: Zone Books.
Deleuze, G., and F. Guattari. 1983. *Anti-Oedipus.* Minneapolis: University of Minnesota Press.
Deleuze, G., and C. Parnet. 1977. *Dialogues*. Paris: Flammarion.
Dews, P. 1995. The crisis of Oedipal identity: The early Lacan and the Frankfurt School. In *Psychoanalysis in Contexts*, ed. A. Elliott and S. Frosh, 53-71. London: Routledge.
Drydyk, J. 1991. Capitalism, Socialism and Civil Society. *Monist* 74 (3): 457-477.
Durkheim, E. 1984. *The Division of Labour in Society*. Trans. W. D. Halls. New York: The Free Press.
Dworkin, R. 1985. *Law's Empire*. Cambridge, Mass.: Harvard University Press.
Eliade, M. 1954. *Cosmos and History*. Princeton: Princeton University Press.
Emerson, R.W. 1983. Politics. In *Essays and Lectures*, ed. J. Porte. New York: Literary Classics of the United States.
Erikson, E. 1950. *Childhood and Society.* New York: Norton.
Fairbairn, W.R.D. 1952. A revised psychopathology of the psychoses and psychoneuroses [1941]. In *Psychoanalytic Studies of the Personality*, 28-58. London: Tavistock, Routledge and Kegan Paul.
Falassi, A., ed. 1987. *Time out of Time*. Albuquerque: University of New Mexico Press.
Finley, M. 1959. *The World of Odysseus*. New York: Viking.
Fish S. 1989. Change, Consequences, Dennis Martinez and the nature of theory. In *Doing What Comes Naturally*, 141-160, 315-341, 372-398. Oxford: Oxford University Press.
Fortes, M. 1969. *Kinship and the Social Order.* Chicago: Aldine.
Foucault, M. 1976. *The Archaeology of Knowledge.* New York: Harper and Row.

Frankfort, H. 1948. *Kingship and the Gods*. Chicago: University of Chicago Press.

Frenkel-Brunswick, E. 1954. Further explorations by a contributor to *The Authoritarian Personality*. In *Studies in the scope and method of the "authoritarian personality"*, ed. R. Christie and M. Jahoda, 226-275. Glencoe, Ill.: Free Press.

Frenkel-Brunswick, E., and R.N. Sanford. 1946. The anti-Semitic personality: a research-report. In *Anti- Semitism: A social disease,* ed. E. Simmel, 96-12. New York: International University Press.

Freud, S. All references are to *The Standard Edition of the Complete Psychological Works of Sigmund Freud*, volumes 1-24, London: Hogarth Press, 1953-1974 (*SE*).

———. 1908. On the sexual theories of children. *SE*, vol. 9, 205-227.

———. 1909. Analysis of a phobia in a five-year-old boy (Little Hans). *SE*, vol. 10, 1-149.

———. 1911. Psychoanalytic notes on an autobiographical account of a case of paranoia (dementia paranoides) (Schreber). *SE*, vol. 12, 1-182.

———. 1912-1913. *Totem and Taboo*. *SE*, vol. 13, 1-162.

———. 1913. The disposition to obsessional neurosis: a contribution to the problem of choice of neurosis. *SE*, vol. 12, 311-326.

———. 1914. On narcissism: an introduction. *SE*, vol. 14, 67-102.

———. 1915. Instincts and their vicissitudes. *SE*, vol. 14, 117-140.

———. 1917a. Mourning and melancholia. *SE*, vol. 14, 237-258.

———. 1917b. On transformations of instinct as exemplified in anal erotism. *SE*, vol. 17, 125-133.

———. 1918. From the history of an infantile neurosis (the 'Wolf man'). *SE*, vol. 17, 3-122.

———. 1919. "A child is being beaten": A contribution to the study of the origin of sexual perversions. *SE*, vol. 17, 175-205.

———. 1920. *Beyond the pleasure principle*. *SE*, vol. 18, 3-64.

———. 1921. *Group psychology and the analysis of the ego*. *SE*, vol. 18, 65-143.

———. 1922. Some neurotic mechanisms in jealousy, paranoia and homosexuality. *SE*, vol. 18, 221-235.

———. 1923a. *The ego and the id*. *SE*, vol. 19, 1-66.

———. 1923b. The infantile genital organization of the libido: an interpretation into the theory of sexuality. *SE*, vol. 19, 139-145.

———. 1924. The economic problem of masochism. *SE*, vol. 19, 155-170.

———. 1926. *Inhibitions, symptoms and anxiety*. *SE*, vol. 20, 75-175.
———. 1930. *Civilization and its discontents*. *SE*, vol. 21, 59-145.
———. 1931. Female sexuality. *SE*, vol. 21, 221-243.
———. 1937. Analysis terminable and interminable. *SE*, vol. 23, 209-253.
———. 1938. Splitting of the ego in the process of defense. *SE*, vol. 23, 275-278.
Fried, Y., and J. Agassi. 1976. *Paranoia: A Study in Diagnosis*. Dordrecht: Reidel.
Friedrich, P. 1978. *The Meaning of Aphrodite*. Chicago: University of Chicago Press.
Fromm, E. 1941. *Escape from Freedom*. New York: Farrar and Rinehart.
———. 1947. *Man for Himself*. New York: Holt, Rinehart and Winston.
———. 1970. The Method and Function of an analytical social psychology, Psychoanalytic characterology and its relevance for social psychology. In *The Crisis of Psychoanalysis: Essays on Freud, Marx and Social Psychology,* 135- 162, 163-189. New York: Holt, Rinehart and Winston.
———. 1975. *The Anatomy of Human Destructiveness*. New York: Fawcett.
———. 1984. *The Working Class in Weimar Germany*. Trans. B. Weinberger, ed. W. Bonss. Warwickshire: Berg.
———. 1991. *The Sane Society*. 2nd ed. London: Routledge.
Gadamer, H. G. 1975. *Truth and Method*. London: Sheed.
———. 1976. *Philosophical Hermeneutics*. Berkeley: University of California Press.
Geertz, C. 1980. *Negara: The Theatre State in nineteenth-century Bali*. Princeton: Princeton University Press.
———. 1985. Centers, Kings and Charisma: Reflections on the symbolics of power. In *Rites of Power,* ed S. Wilentz. Philadelphia. University of Pennsylvania Press.
———. 1993. Local Knowledge: Fact and Law in Comparative Perspective. In *Local Knowledge,* 167-235. London: Fontana.
Gilligan, C. 1982. *In a Different Voice: Psychological Theory and Women's Development*. Cambridge, Mass.: Harvard University Press.
Gilman, S. 1995. *Franz Kafka, The Jewish Patient*. New York: Routledge.
Girard, R. 1977. *Violence and the Sacred*. Baltimore: Johns Hopkins University Press.
———. 1986. *The Scapegoat*. London: Athlone.

———. 1987. *Things Hidden since the Foundation of the World.* London: Athlone.

———. 1988. Camus's stranger retired. In *To double Business Bound,* 9-36. London: Athlone.

Grunberger, B. 1979. *Narcissism.* Trans. J. S. Diamanti. New York: International Universities Press.

Grunberger, B., and P. Dessuant. 1997. *Narcissisme, Christianisme, Antisemitisme.* Arles: Actes Sud.

Guizot , F. 1985. *Histoire de la civilisation.* Ed. P. Rosanvallon. Paris: Hachette.

Habermas, J. 1974. Hegel's Critique of the French Revolution. In *Theory and Practice,* tr. J. Viertel, 121-141. London: Heinemann.

———. 1977. A Review of Gadamer's Truth and Method. In *Understanding and Social Inquiry,* ed. F. Dallmayr and T. McCarthy. Notre Dame: University of Notre Dame Press.

———. 1979. *Communication and the Evolution of Society.* London: Heinemann.

———. 1984. *The Theory of Communicative Action.* Vol. 1. Cambridge: Polity.

———. 1987. *The Theory of Communicative Action.* Vol. 2. Cambridge: Polity.

———. 1988. *On the Logic of the Social Sciences.* Cambridge, Mass.: MIT Press.

———. 1990a. *Moral Consciousness and Communicative action.* Cambridge, Mass.: Polity.

———. 1990b. Morality and Ethical Life: Does Hegel's Critique of Kant apply to discourse ethics? In *Moral Consciousness and Communicative Action,* 195-217. Cambridge Mass: MIT Press.

———. 1992a. *Autonomy and Solidarity.* London: Verso.

———. 1992b. *Postmetaphysical Thinking.* Cambridge, Mass.: MIT Press.

———. 1992c. *The Structural Transformation of the Public Sphere.* Cambridge: Polity.

———. 1992d. Further Reflections of the Public Sphere, Concluding Remarks. In *Habermas and the Public Sphere,* ed. C. Calhoun, 421-481. Cambridge, Mass.: MIT.

———. 1993. Remarks on Discourse Ethics. In *Justification and Application.* Cambridge Mass.: MIT Press.

———. 1994. *The Past as Future.* Cambridge: Polity.

———. 1995. Reconciliation through the public use of reason: remarks on John Rawls's Political Liberalism. *Journal of Philosophy* 92: 109-131.

Hardimon, M. 1992. The Project of Reconciliation: Hegel's Social Philosophy. *Philosophy and Public Affairs* 21: 165-196.

Hegel G.W.F. 1942. *Philosophy of Right*. Trans. T.M. Knox. Oxford: Oxford University Press.

———. 1944. *The Philosophy of History*. Trans. J. Sibree. New York: Willey.

———. 1969. *Science of Logic*. Trans. A.V. Miller. London: Allen and Unwin.

———. 1971. *Philosophy of Mind*. Trans. A.V. Miller. Oxford: Oxford University Press.

———. 1975a. *Natural Law*. Trans. T.M. Knox. Philadelphia: University of Pennsylvania Press.

———. 1975b. *Hegel's Logic*. Trans. W. Wallace. Oxford: Oxford University Press.

———. 1975c. *Lectures on the Philosophy of World-History: Introduction*. Trans. H.B. Nisbet. Cambridge: Cambridge University Press.

———. 1977a. *The Difference Between Fichte's and Schelling's System of Philosophy*. Trans. H.S. Harris and W. Cerf. Albany: State University of New York Press.

———. 1977b. *Faith and Knowledge*. Trans. W. Cerf and H.S. Harris. Albany: State University of New York Press.

———. 1977c. *The Phenomenology of Spirit*. Trans. A.V. Miller. Oxford: Oxford University Press.

———. 1979. *System of Ethical Life* and *First Philosophy of Spirit*. Trans. H.S. Harris and W. Cerf. Albany: State University of New York Press.

———. 1983. *Philosophie des Rechts: Die Vorlesung von 1819 / 1820 in einer Nachschrift*. Ed. D. Henrich. Frankfurt am Main: Suhrkamp.

———. 1985. *Introduction to the Lectures on the History of Philosophy*. Trans. T.M. Knox. and A.V. Miller. Oxford: Oxford University Press.

———. 1988. *Lectures on the Philosophy of Religion: The lecture of 1827*. Ed. P. C. Hodgson. Berkeley: University of California Press.

———. 1995. *Lectures on the History of Philosophy*. Vol. 2. Trans. E.S. Haldane and F.H. Simpson. Lincoln: University of Nebraska Press.

de-Heusch, L. 1987. Pour une dialectique de la sacralité du pouvoir (1962). In *Écrits sur la royauté sacrée*. Bruxelles: Editions de l'université de Bruxelles.

Honneth, A. 1995. *The struggle for Recognition*. Cambridge: Polity Press.

Horkheimer, M. 1949. Authoritarianism and the Family Today. In *The Family and its Function,* ed. R.N. Anshen, 359-374. New York: Harper.

———. 1950. The lessons of fascism. In *Tensions that Cause Wars,* ed. H. Cantril. Urbana: University of Illinois Press.

———. 1972. Authority and the Family. In *Critical Theory,* 47-129. New York: Continuum.

Ionescu, G. and E. Gellner, eds. 1969. *Populism*. London: Weidenfeld.

James, E.O. 1959. *The cult of the Mother Goddess*. London: Thames and Hudson.

Jones, E. 1951. The Psychology of Quislingism. In *Essays in Applied Psychoanalysis*. Vol. 2. London: Hogarth.

Jung, C. G. 1966. *Two Essays on Analytical Psychology*. Princeton: Princeton University Press.

———. 1982. *Aspects of the Feminine.* Princeton: Princeton University Press.

Kafka, F. 1953. *Letter to his Father*. Trans. E. Kaiser and E. Wilkins. New York: Schocken.

Kantorowicz, E. H. 1997. *The King's Two Bodies*. Princeton University Press.

Kaufmann, W. 1970. The Hegel Myth and its Method. In *Hegel's Political Philosophy*. New York: Atherton Press.

———. 1974. *Nietzsche: Philosopher, Psychologist, Antichrist.* Princeton: Princeton University Press.

Kernberg, O. 1974. Contrasting viewpoints regarding the nature and psychoanalytic treatment of narcissistic personalities: a preliminary communication. *Journal of the American Psychoanalytic Association* 22:255-267.

———. 1995. *Love Relations*. New Haven: Yale University Press.

Kershaw, I., and M. Lewin, eds. 1997. *Stalinism and Nazism, Dictatorships in Comparison*. Cambridge: Cambridge University Press.

Klein, M. 1928. Early stages of the Oedipus Complex. In *Love, Guilt and Reparation and other works 1921-1945,* 186-199. London: Virago.

———. 1935. A contribution to the psychogenesis of manic-depressive states. In *The selected Melanie Klein,* ed. J. Mitchell, 115-145. Harmondsworth: Penguin.

———. 1940. Mourning and its relation to manic-depressive states. In

The selected Melanie Klein, ed. J. Mitchell, 146-175. Harmondsworth: Penguin.

———. 1945. The Oedipus Complex in Light of Early Anxieties. In *Love, Guilt and Reparation and other works 1921-1945,* 370-420. London: Virago.

———. 1946. Notes on some schizoid mechanisms. In *The selected Melanie Klein*, ed. J. Mitchell, 175-201. Harmondsworth: Penguin.

———. 1948. On the theory of anxiety and guilt. In *Envy and Gratitude and other works 1946-1963,* 25-43. London: Virago.

———. 1950. *The Psychoanalysis of Children.* London: Hogarth.

———. 1952. Some Theoretical Conclusions Regarding the Emotional Life of the Infant. In *Envy and Gratitude and other works 1946-1963,* 61-94. London: Virago.

———. 1957. Envy and Gratitude. In *Envy and Gratitude and other works 1946-1963,* 176-236. London: Virago.

Kogan, N. 1956. Authoritarianism and repression. *Journal of Abnormal and Social Psychology* 53: 34-37.

Kohut, H. 1971. *The Analysis of the Self.* New York: International Universities Press.

———. 1973. Thoughts on Narcissism and Narcissistic Rage. *The Psychoanalytic Study of the Child* 27:360-400.

———. 1984. *How Does Analysis Cure?* Chicago: University of Chicago Press.

———. 1985a. On leadership. In *Self Psychology and the Humanities,* ed. C. B. Strozier, 82. New York: Norton.

———. 1985b. Forms and Transformations of Narcissism. In *Self Psychology and the Humanities*, ed. C. B. Strozier, 97-123. New York: Norton.

Kuhn, T. 1970. *The Structure of Scientific Revolutions*. 2nd. ed. Chicago: University of Chicago Press.

Lacan, J. 1992. *The Ethics of Psychoanalysis*. London: Routledge.

Laclau, E., and C. Mouffe. 1994. *Hegemony and Socialist Strategy.* London: Verso.

Lasswell, H. D. 1951. Democratic Character. In *The Political Writings of Harold D. Lasswell,* 465-525. Illinois: The Free Press.

Leach, E. R. 1976. *Culture and Communication.* Cambridge: Cambridge University Press.

Lefort, C. 1986. *The Logic of Totalitarianism*. In: *The Political Forms of Modern Society*, 273-292. Cambridge: MIT Press.

Legendre, P. 1989. *Le Crime du Corporal Lortie, Traité sur le Père.*

Paris: Fayard.
———. 1992. *Les enfants du Texte. Étude sur la fonction parentale des États*. Paris: Fayard.
______. 1996. *L'inestimable objet de la transmission.* Paris: Fayard.
Lévêque, P. 1997. *Introduction aux premièrs religions, Bêtes, dieux et hommes*. Paris: Le livre de poche.
Lewin, M. 1997. Stalin in the mirror of the other. In *Stalinism and Nazism, Dictatorships in Comparison,* ed. I. Kershaw and M. Lewin, 107-135. Cambridge: Cambridge University Press.
Lipset, S.M. 1960. *Political Man*. New York: Doubleday.
Machiavelli, N. 1994. Discourses. In *Selected Political Writings*, ed. D. Wootton. Indianapolis: Hackett.
MacIntyre, A.1985. *After Virtue*. 2nd ed. London: Duckworth.
———. 1988. The Rationality of Traditions. In *Whose Justice? Which Rationality?*, 349-370. Notre Dame: University of Notre Dame Press.
MacRae, D. 1969. Populism as an ideology. In *Populism,* ed. E. Gellner and G. Ionescu, 153-165. London: Weidenfeld.
Magnus, B. 1988. The Use and Abuse of *The Will to Power*. In *Reading Nietzsche,* ed. C.S. Solomon and K.M. Higgins, 218-235. New York and Oxford: Oxford University Press.
Mahler, M. 1979. On Human Symbiosis and the Vicissitudes of Individuation. *Selected Papers* Vol. 2, 77-98. New York: Aronson.
Makkreel, R. A. 1991. Reinterpreting the historical world. *The Monist*: 149-164.
Marcuse, H. The Obsolescence of the Freudian concept of Man. In *Five Lectures*, 44-61. Boston: Beacon.
Marinetti, F. T. 1971. *Selected Writings,* ed. R. W. Flint. New York: Farrar, Straus and Giroux.
Marx, K. 1992. *Early Writings*. Harmondsworth: Penguin.
Mason, A. 1993. *Explaining Political Disagreement*. Cambridge: Cambridge University Press.
Mead, G. H. 1934. *Mind, Self and Society*. Chicago: Chicago University Press.
———. 1964. *Selected Writings*. Chicago: University of Chicago Press.
Meltzer, D. 1968. Terror, persecution, dread - a dissection of paranoid anxieties. *International Journal of Psychoanalysis* 49: 396.
———. 1973. *Sexual States of Mind.* Perthshire, Scotland: Clunie Press
Mendelsohn, E., ed. 1997. *Essential papers on Jews and the Left.* New York: New York University Press.
Miller, A. 1981. *The Drama of the Gifted Child.* New York: Basic

Books.
———. 1983. *For Your Own Good.* New York: Farrar, Straus, Giroux.
Mitscherlich, A. 1969. *Society without the Father.* London: Tavistock.
Mosse, G. L. 1985. *Nationalism and Sexuality.* Madison: The University of Wisconsin Press.
Mueller, G.H. 1982. Socialism and Capitalism in the Work of Max Weber. *British Journal of Sociology* 33: 151-171.
Mussen, P. H., J. J. Conger, J. Kagan, and A.C. Huston 1990. *Child Development and Personality.* 7th ed. New York: Harper and Row.
Neumann, E. 1955. *The Great Mother: An Analysis of the Archetype.* London: Routledge and Kegan Paul.
———. 1994. *The Fear of the Feminine.* Princeton: Princeton University Press.
Nietzsche, F. 1967a. *On the Genealogy of Morals.* Trans. W. Kaufmann. New York: Vintage.
———. 1967b. *Ecce Homo.* Trans. W. Kaufmann. New York: Vintage.
———.1968a. *Twilight of the Idols* and *The Anti-Christ.* Trans. R.J. Hollingdale. Harmondsworth: Penguin.
———. 1968b. *The Will to Power.* Trans. W. Kaufmann. New York: Vintage.
———. 1969. *Thus Spoke Zarathustra.* Trans. R. J. Hollingdale. Harmondsworth: Penguin.
———. 1973. *Beyond Good and Evil.* Trans. R.J. Hollingdale. Harmondsworth: Penguin.
———. 1974. *The Gay Science.* Trans. W. Kaufmann. New York: Vintage.
———. 1994. *Human, All Too Human.* Trans. M. Faber. Harmondsworth: Penguin
Odajnyk, V. W. 1976. *Jung and Politics.* New York: Harper and Row.
O'Neill, J., ed. 1996. *Hegel's Dialectic of Desire and Recognition.* Albany: State University of New York Press.
Ostrogorski, M. 1982. *Democracy and the Organization of Political Parties.* Ed. S.M. Lipset. New Brunswick: Transaction Books.
Pateman, C. 1987. Feminist Critiques of the Public/Private Dichotomy. In *Feminism and Equality,* ed. A. Phillips, 103-126. Oxford: Basil Blackwell.
Pinkard, T. 1994. *Hegel's Phenomenology: The Sociality of Reason.* Cambridge: Cambridge University Press.
Rawls, J. 1971. *A Theory of Justice.* Harvard: Harvard University Press.
———. 1993. *Political Liberalism.* New York: Columbia University

Press.
———. 1995. Reply to Habermas. *Jour. of Phil.* 92:132-180.
Reich, W. 1970. *The Mass Psychology of Fascism.* Trans. V.R. Carfagno. New York: Farrar, Straus and Giroux.
———. 1972. *Sex-Pol Essays 1929-1934.* New York: Vintage.
Ritter, J. 1982. *Hegel and the French Revolution: Essays on the Philosophy of Right.* Cambridge, Mass.: MIT Press.
Robins, R. S., and J. M. Post. 1988. *Political Paranoia.* New Haven: Yale University Press.
Roheim, G. 1950. *Psychoanalysis and Anthropology.* New York: International Universities Press.
Rorty, R. 1980. *Philosophy and the Mirror of Nature.* Oxford: Blackwell.
Rosenfeld, H. 1971. A clinical approach to the psychoanalytic theory of the life and death instincts: an investigation into the aggressive aspects of narcissism. *Int. J. Psycho-Anal. 52*: 169-178.
———. 1990. *Impasse and Interpretation.* London: Routledge.
Rumpf, M. 1993. 'Mystical Aura': Imagination and the Reality of the "Maternal" in Horkheimer's Writings. In *On Max Horkheimer,* ed. S. Benhabib, W. Bonns and J. M. John, 309-334. Cambridge, Mass.: MIT Press.
Sartre, J. P. 1947. *Baudelaire.* Paris: Gallimard.
———.1949. *Baudelaire.* Trans. M. Turnell. London: Horizon.
Schimmel, P., and R. Ferguson, eds. 1998. *Out of Actions: between performance and the object, 1949-1979.* London: Thames and Hudson.
Schmitt, C. 1996. *The Concept of the Political.* Chicago: University of Chicago Press.
Schnepel, B. 1991. Continuity despite and through death: regicide and royal shrines among the Shilluk of southern Sudan. *Africa* 61(1): 40-70.
Schochet, G. J. 1975. *Patriarchalism in Political Thought.* New York: Basic Books.
Scholem, G. 1974. *On the Kabbalah and its Symbolism.* New York: Shocken.
Schorske, C. 1973. Politics and Patricide in Freud's *Interpretation of Dreams. The American Historical Review* 78(1): 328-47.
Searle, J. 1969. *Speech Acts.* Cambridge: Cambridge University Press.
Segal, H. 1973. *Introduction to the Work of Melanie Klein.* London: Hogarth Press.

———. 1986. Notes on Symbol Formation. In *The Work of Hanna Segal.* London: Free Association Books.
———. 1997. *Psychoanalysis, Literature and War*. London: Routledge.
Shapiro, Y. 1991. *The Road to Power*. Albany: State University of New York Press.
Shoham, S. G. 1978. *Salvation through the Gutters*. Washington, D.C.: Hemisphere
———. 1979. *The Myth of Tantalus.* Queensland: University of Queensland Press.
Silone, I. 1964. *The School for Dictators*. London: Gollancz.
Singer, P. 1973. *Democracy and Disobedience*. Oxford: Oxford University Press.
Slater, P. E. 1992. *The Glory of Hera.* Princeton: Princeton University Press.
Staël, Madame de. 1818. *Considerations sur la Revolution Francaise.* Paris: Charpentier.
Storr, A. 1991. *Human Destructiveness*. London: Routledge.
Taylor, C. 1989. *Sources of the Self.* Cambridge: Cambridge University Press.
———. 1991. Hegel's ambiguous legacy for modern liberalism. In *Hegel and Legal Theory,* ed. D. Cornell, D.G. Carlson and M. Rosenfeld. London: Routledge.
———. 1995. *Philosophical Arguments*. Cambridge, Mass.: Harvard University Press.
Theweleit, K. 1987. *Male Fantasies*. Vol. 1. Cambridge: Polity.
———. 1989. *Male Fantasies*. Vol. 2. Cambridge: Polity.
Tocqueville, A de. 1955. *The Old Regime and the French Revolution.* Trans. S. Gilbert. New York: Doubleday.
———. 1987. Chapters and notes for his unfinished books on the French Revolution. In *The Two Tocquevilles, Herve and Alexis de Tocqueville on the coming of the French Revolution,* ed. R. R. Palmer. Princeton: Princeton University Press.
Tunick, M. 1992. *Hegel's political philosophy*. Princeton: Princeton University Press.
Turner, V. 1969. *The Ritual Process.* Ithaca: Cornell University Press.
———. 1982. *From Ritual to Theater*. New York: Performing Arts Journal Publications.
———. 1985. Images of Anti-Temporality. In *On the Edge of the Bush,* 227-245. Tuscon: The University of Arizona Press.
Vargas Llosa, M. 1986. *The Real Life of Alejandro Mayta.* London:

Faber and Faber.

Walker, N., and M. Hough, eds. 1988. *Public Attitudes to Sentencing.* Aldershot: Gower.

Walzer, M. 1994. *Thin and Thick.* Notre Dame: Notre Dame University Press.

Warren, M. 1988. *Nietzsche and Political Thought.* Cambridge, Mass.: MIT Press.

Wiggerhaus, R. 1994. *The Frankfurt School.* Boston: Polity.

Wiles, P. 1969. A syndrome, not a doctrine. In *Populism,* ed. E. Gellner and G. Ionescu, 166-179. London: Weidenfeld.

Williams, B. 1993. *Ethics and the Limits of Philosophy.* London: Fontana.

Winch, P. 1970. Understanding a Primitive Society. In *Rationality*, ed. B. Wilson. Oxford: Blackwell.

Winnicott, D.W. 1951. Transitional Objects and transitional phenomena. In *Through Paediatrics to Psycho-Analysis, collected papers,* 229-242. New York: Brunner.

———. 1960. Ego distortion in terms of True and False self. In *The Maturational Processes and the Facilitating Environment,* 140-152. London : Karnac.

———. 1965. Some Thoughts of the Meaning of the Word Democracy. In *The Family and Individual Development,* 155-169. London: Tavistock.

———. 1966. The absence of a sense of guilt. In *Deprivation and Delinquency,* ed. C. Winnicott, R. Shepherd and M. Davis, 106-112. London: Tavistock.

———. 1991. *Playing and Reality.* London: Routledge.

Wittgenstein L. 1974. *On Certainty.* Oxford: Oxford University Press.

Wood, A. 1990. *Hegel's Ethical Thought.* Cambridge: Cambridge University Press.

Worseley, P. M. 1955. Totemism in a changing Society. *American Anthropologist* 57: 851-861

Zizek, S. 1991. *For they know not what they do.* London: Verso.

INDEX

Note: Some entries that appear throughout the book, such as Sigmund Freud, Georg Wilhelm Friedrich Hegel, misrecognition and recognition, are not listed in the Index.